DO YOU HAVE A DIFFICULT HUSBAND?

1. Are you tired of "being patient" with your husband's behavior? ☐ Yes ☐ No

2. Are you at a loss as to how to change your husband's behavior without threats or arguing? ☐ Yes ☐ No

3. Are you disrespected by your husband? ☐ Yes ☐ No

4. Does his anger lead to arguments? ☐ Yes ☐ No

5. Do you withdraw, walk on eggshells, or avoid talking about things because of your husband's anger? ☐ Yes ☐ No

6. Is your husband unhappy but unwilling to work on making things better? ☐ Yes ☐ No

7. Has your husband emotionally withdrawn from your relationship? ☐ Yes ☐ No

8. Does he only spend time with you when he "has to"? ☐ Yes ☐ No

9. Is your husband selfish about money, sex, time, or helping with child or house care? ☐ Yes ☐ No

10. Do you struggle with thoughts about divorcing or breaking up? ☐ Yes ☐ No

Each question relates to the relationship problems of women with angry, avoidant, unhappy, or selfish husbands. The more of the questions that you have answered "yes" to, the more you can improve your relationship by making the kinds of changes in this book.

WHAT TO DO WHEN HE WON'T CHANGE

SAVING YOUR MARRIAGE OR RELATIONSHIP WHEN HE IS ANGRY, SELFISH, UNHAPPY, OR AVOIDS YOU

JACK ITO, PH.D.

DEDICATION

This book is dedicated to my clients who have hung in there in their relationships while other people were jumping ship. Thank you for giving my work meaning and for helping me to keep my belief in the importance of love and commitment.

CONTENTS

Self-Esteem● Family Harmony

WARNING—DISCLAIMER

This book was written to provide general guidance to women who have angry, avoidant, unhappy and selfish husbands. It was not written to provide guidance for women with physically abusive, violent, or potentially violent husbands or boyfriends. Any person needing assistance with such a situation should consult professional help, including psychological, supportive, and legal services.

A good relationship does not happen quickly. Anyone who decides to have a good long term relationship must work on it continuously, both addressing concerns as well as promoting positive communication and togetherness. This book addresses a small, but important aspect of some long term relationships. It can't be used as a comprehensive manual of relating. No book could conceivably offer all that is needed to guarantee a positive long term relationship. Human interaction is simply too complex.

Great care has been taken to make this manual as complete and accurate as possible regarding its content. However, there *may be mistakes*, both typographical and in content. Therefore this book should be used only as a general guide and not as the ultimate source of managing relational differences. Furthermore, this book is current only up until the printing date.

In a book of this sort it is not possible to take into account individual differences that influence the success or failure of these methods. The author and publisher have no responsibility to any person or entity in regard to loss or damage caused, or thought to have been caused, directly or indirectly by the contents of this book.

If you are not in agreement with this disclaimer, you may return the book to the seller for a full refund.

INTRODUCTION

Why do some boyfriends and husbands who *were* nice, talkative, affectionate, thoughtful, and happy become completely different? What accounts for this change from early to mid relationship? And, when their behavior is obviously causing problems, why don't they change back to the way they were before?

The simple answer is that after receiving a commitment from a woman, the *motivation* for their behavior changes. Different motivations equal different behavior. A man who has what he wants puts his energy into other things. While that is an oversimplification, it makes clear why men become ready to "change" or "reform" when threatened with separation or divorce, and why they return to their previous motivation of getting you to commit (or re-commit) to the relationship. They become motivated by desperation to avoid losing what they thought they securely had. Men hate rejection worse than they hate a bad relationship. Although men will sometimes be the ones to end a relationship, it is usually only after they feel hopelessly rejected or after they find another woman who they value more.

There are a large group of single men who try hard, but don't have the skills to get into a long term relationship. Most of these men are too inept to get past the first date unless they find an equally inept woman. There is another group of men who have the skills for starting a relationship, and for making a good emotional connection, but unfortunately have difficulty maintaining a long term relationship. For them, the length of their relationship is related to the "patience" of the women they are in a relationship with. *This book was written for these women*, who are being "patient" with their husbands (for the sake of brevity, I will use the word "husband" with the meaning that he is committed to a long-term relationship, regardless of the presence of a marriage license).

You are married to (committed to) a man who is *able* to have as good an emotional connection with you as he had before. He doesn't have an antisocial personality disorder, and he is not severely lacking in social skills. He knows how to get along with people when he wants too. You have had good experiences with him, even if you are not having them now. You are continuing to be with him because you know the man you fell in love with is still inside him. He is not itching for a divorce, and in fact, would be very upset if you made a move to end the relationship. In some way that you may not understand, he needs you and loves you.

Even if you have not yet threatened to end your relationship, you may have a husband who is alert to any threats to your relationship—except for those coming from his own behavior. If so, he probably has jealous and/or anxious behaviors like questioning you and checking up on you. Reassuring such men works temporarily, but only temporarily. Their behavior can make you tired, frustrated, and increasingly distant. They can push you so far away emotionally that they make it more likely they will lose you. In fact, although you are still physically with him you may have already emotionally left him.

If your husband cares so much about your relationship, then why does he make it so hard for you to love him? Why is he pushing you away if he is afraid of losing you? We will take a close look at the reasons for these behaviors in this book. With such understanding, we will then get about helping your husband to change. In most cases, like a child with a cavity, he will need help, but he will not want it. Your job will be to learn how to overcome his resistance, and help him to change, for his sake as well as your own. Helping him to love you better is the correct response to his behavior because it saves his relationship as much as your own. Being "patient" with his harmful behavior would not be loving. Eventually, it would damage his relationship with you even more. Patience that hurts another is not patience—it is negligence.

If you think your only solution for maintaining your sanity and your happiness is to get out of your relationship, you have come to the point that many people do when they don't know what to do. They come to the verge of either burning out or bailing out. It has been my great pleasure to help many men and women in this very situation. I have seen love rekindled in many relationships that people thought were long past rescuing. I have also worked with many men whose wives left them or were on the verge of leaving them because of the kinds of behaviors talked about in this book. These men were very motivated to have their wives back and were willing to change themselves in order to have their wives back. But like most difficult men, they did not know how. Only with the assistance of their loving wives could they make lasting changes.

Motivating your husband and knowing how to help him when he is motivated are what you need to make change happen. These can't be accomplished merely by threats of leaving or separating. If you leave him or threaten to, he may be motivated to change, but he still won't know how. He will beg, plead, and suppress his emotions to get you back, but he still won't know how to change. And if he fails to get you to come back, you will get to see all the ugly emotions he was holding in. Whether it's threats or suicide attempts, it's not a pretty sight. Don't be fooled by men who seem to have reformed overnight.

Threatening to leave brings immediate change but not lasting change. It is also damaging to your relationship in the long run. The main reason for this is that when women threaten to leave, men feel more insecure (just as women would in the same situation). And, insecurity is what accounts for most of men's (and women's) bad behavior. So, if you threaten to leave your husband, he will have the *urge* to do many insecure things (get jealous, control you, withdraw, become secretive, etc.) while at the same time trying desperately to control himself and win your approval. The internal conflict creates a high level of stress which can make him emotionally fall apart so much that he either destroys your relationship or becomes so pitiable that you take him back without any significant change.

How can you motivate your husband to change without making him more insecure? I believe that the answer to this question has two parts. The first is for you to change the way you see your husband. You especially need to stop seeing him as someone who cares only about himself. That simply doesn't fit the facts, although it might seem to fit his behavior. Much better, and closer to the truth, is to see your husband as a man who loves you, and who cares about the relationship. Although he doesn't want to lose you, he uses *minimally effective* skills to hold onto you and to get along. I say *minimally effective*, because like a lazy maid, they do work to some extent. You are, after all, still with him. The second part of the answer then is to make his bad behaviors ineffective (but without leaving him). They must utterly fail with you before he will do something else. A man shouldn't get his way by having a tantrum or by crying any more than a child should. You must learn how to take corrective action at these times. For him, it will be an abrupt wake-up call when his bad behaviors no longer work with you. I remember when I was a child, my father had an old radio alarm clock. It no longer played the radio, but the alarm still worked. Because of loose connections, to set the alarm, he had to wiggle it and jiggle it for five minutes every night. I asked him why he didn't get a new one. Of course, you know the answer—because it still worked. By making sure that your husband's bad behaviors no longer work, he will be ready to get some new ones.

The unwritten but closely followed rule that people live by is to continue to do whatever works, even if it works only a little. This explains why most people don't excel, but why they do get by. Like someone who is playing a slot machine, a one in 10 payoff keeps them playing, although the other 9 plays are costly and result in an overall loss. Nine times out of 10, your husband's behavior may make things worse for him. But if he can get satisfaction, avoid a problem, get attention, or get control one time in 10, it will do. Do you know the best way to get someone to stop playing a slot machine? To set it so that it never pays off. Zero. Zilch. Put an "out of order" sign on the slot machine and no one will put money in it. Even the most addicted gambler won't put a quarter in a slot machine whose plug has been pulled. You are your husband's slot machine (I know I'm treading very dangerously here! *Please* read the next sentence).

You are not responsible for your husband's behavior. And he did not learn his bad behavior from you. But, he continues to do that bad behavior because it is what he knows how to do and because it works for him. With you. A little. The proof is that you are still with him. This book will teach you how to make his behavior no longer work for him while at the same time, you help him to be successful with you. And he wants to be successful with you. You have heard it said that behind every successful man is a supportive woman. I believe it's true. These women don't behave like doormats. They not only know how to manage themselves, they help their husbands to manage, too. I will help you to be successful in dealing with your husband's behavior so that he can have more success with you. I will coach you to go for the win-win.

When we start with the assumption that he wants to have a relationship with you, and loves you, but goes about it in the wrong way, it becomes easier to love him and help him. He is more misguided than monster. You have an opportunity for relationship growth. It can be a very positive and exciting time. At this moment the light is focused on you, and the ball is in your court. What are you going to do?

I am sorry things had to get so difficult for you before you got to this point. But, your desire to end your pain is actually our ally. If you were a little less miserable, you might let things drift on for years when you and your husband could actually have so much more here and now. With each other.

I have been counseling and coaching people since 1994. In all that time, I have not seen a relationship that could not be improved. And I have *never* recommended divorce. Be assured, that in these pages is help for your relationship. Although many of the things you will need to do are not easy, they are easier than what you fear—living an unhappy life that ends with regret. There is no need for that. So, come along, and learn how *not* to control your husband, *not* to fight your husband, *not* to endure your husband, but how to *help* your husband, your relationship, and yourself.

Section One: Preparing for Change

"The only man who makes no mistakes is the man who never does anything." Eleanor Roosevelt

1

UNDERSTANDING DIFFICULT MEN

John starts shouting almost before he closes the front door. Whatever he's got to say, has been building all day. As he shouts, red faced, squint eyed, scowling at his wife Mary, she says nothing. John even pauses at times to wait for her response. Still she says nothing. Finally, he stops and asks her if she isn't going to say anything.

Mary calmly replies, "Yes, I am. I was waiting for you to finish so I could make sure I heard your important points." John looks surprised, expectant. Mary then restates the points she heard her husband make. She doesn't defend herself against his accusations, she doesn't try to explain her behavior, and she doesn't give counter-arguments. If he starts shouting again, she won't try to calm him down. When he stops, she restates his points again. Feeling understood, but getting no answers, John will likely demand them from his wife.

"I will answer all your questions," she says, "but not right now. We can set a time when you and I are both calm and I will answer everything. Whenever you come at me, shouting like that, I will listen, but I won't give you answers until we are both calm." (By saying "we" Mary avoids sounding accusatory, and shares the problem).

3

"To hell with that!" John replies, and storms off. For the first time in 5 years, John's shouting does not lead to an argument. His wife has taken control. What would seem like a failure for many women is a victory for Mary. And things are starting to change.

Mary is one of the many women I coach each day. They all have two things in common: 1) they love their husbands, and 2) their husbands are driving them crazy. Mary is learning how to stop her husband's bad behavior from being successful with her—one of two keys to changing his behavior. The other key will be to help him learn how to get what he wants (in this case, answers) in a way that actually builds the relationship. The first week of change will be hard, but not as hard as continuing to live with John the way things are. If Mary continues to put up with John's behavior without making changes, there will be no relationship left to save. And on this first day of change, she has done great! She is eager to write about it in her success journal.

Mary, and many women like her, are learning with a relationship coach how to make changes in their relationship. In no longer playing the role of victim, Mary is initiating change rather than waiting for it. Women like Mary will still have a backup plan of leaving, if changing things doesn't work. But, what becomes apparent again and again, is that their husbands do still love them, and change is possible.

I also work with many men whose wives have separated from them. They don't want to lose their wives, and know they must change, but don't know how. My heart goes out to these men who feel hurt, rejected, angry, and sad all at the same time as they try to figure out what to do—how to change. How to stop their wives from divorcing them. I help them to make radical changes. When their wives are willing to help, they change much faster. You can help your husband too, without needing to separate. It will be my privilege to teach you how, in this book.

What is a Difficult Husband/Boyfriend/Partner?

The problems in your relationship are easy enough for you to see. Perhaps you and your husband ("husband" meaning the man you are committed to, marriage license or not) don't talk anymore, or talk a lot but without concern for each other. Maybe you get treated like everything except a wife ("wife" meaning a woman with a lifelong commitment to the relationship). You get treated like a parent, or like a child, like a subordinate, like an enemy, or even like someone who doesn't really matter. Your husband may do this with anger, withdrawal, neglect, suspiciousness, or indifference.

As different as difficult men's presentations are, they have one thing in common—they cause emotional pain for their partners. If your husband's behavior doesn't hurt you as much as it used to, it means that you have found a way to block the pain so that it feels like less of a problem. The hurt has moved from the surface to deep inside you. This turns out to be both helpful and harmful. While it's good not to always be aware of your pain, it also takes away from the urgency to make changes. Although nobody wants to feel pain, it is that ability that saves us physically, and can save our relationships, too.

Pain works by focusing our attention on what is damaging us physically or emotionally. That's good, because if we didn't notice something that was hurting us, we might not do anything about it until severe damage was done. Ever burn your hand on a hot stove? If you did, I bet you didn't leave it there very long. You didn't need to think about it or wonder what was the best thing to do. You jerked it away immediately. And that's what pain does, whether physical or emotional—it makes us want to pull away immediately. If our actions are effective, we are only slightly injured and heal soon. If our actions are not effective, the pain continues, and more and more damage is done. Failing to deal with physical pain can result in a lost life. Failing to deal with emotional pain can result in a lost relationship.

Because pain is always shouting "Danger, danger!" the most natural reactions are the ones which put an end to the pain most quickly. In relationships, these natural reactions are *fighting* (to stop someone from causing us pain), *running away* (to prevent their being able to cause us pain), and *shutting down* (to make their mistreatment more bearable). These natural reactions are more or less effective in putting an end to immediate danger. The more pain someone feels, the more intensely they will take one of these three courses. You can measure your own level of emotional pain by noticing how much you have these reactions.

Understanding these natural reactions to pain helps to explain your own reactions, but may also explain those of your husband. His fighting or other attempts to control you, his behaviors that let him avoid you, or his tuning you out may be his way of dealing with pain. You don't have to be the cause of his pain to see these reactions in him. A man who is unhappy for any reason can bring these behaviors into the relationship. He can also bring the pain of a past relationship into his relationship with you (emotional baggage). He can even do these things to prevent pain, if he has had really bad experiences before, and anticipates having them again.

Whatever the cause and no matter how hurt you feel, if your husband tries to control you, avoid you, or shuts down, it's not because his main goal is to hurt you. Someone who just wants to hurt you is a psychopath, a crazy man, who should be locked up. That's *not* your husband. Your husband may do things differently from you, but they are for the same emotional reasons. Basically, he is a human being with the same needs as you. It's not hurting you that he wants. He wants to put an end to his own pain, prevent whatever he sees as dangerous, and get his needs met. Same as you. He will attempt to control, escape, or shut down in order to do that. His methods are the problem. To fix your relationship, you will especially need to stop him from continuing to use methods that hurt you. And, you will need to help him to be more effective in getting his needs met and in having a good relationship with you. These things are not beyond his ability—they are what many other men already do. He doesn't need a new personality—he needs a behavior adjustment. *He* needs it, but you will benefit too.

You also may be doing things now that unintentionally hurt your husband. And it's not because you are a psychopath either. It's because you are trying to end the hurt for yourself. Maybe for some of the same reasons. Learning more effective methods for stopping your pain, which don't push your husband away, will also make it easier for him to have a closer relationship with you. There are simply better ways to deal with relationship problems and emotional pain than what you and your husband are doing now. As long as you are patient with yourself, you can learn the exact changes you need to make. And as long as you set the right conditions, your husband will learn, too.

Not Sure If You Still Love Him?

Have you noticed that you don't love your husband as much as you used to? If things are really bad, it may feel like you don't love him anymore at all. Before you decide that means your relationship is over, consider one thing. When you shut down your feelings to protect yourself from pain, you shut down *all* your feelings. When you block pain, you won't be able to feel as happy, as sad, as mad, as worried, or as in love. Your love for your husband didn't disappear, it got suppressed. It's locked away with your other feelings. You can sense this is true because your emotional "safe" has holes in it. Your feelings leak out. Sometimes unexpectedly, and sometimes when you see or hear something that reminds you of what matters to you most. Just seeing a picture of a couple holding hands may make you cry or suddenly become angry. When you work on improving your relationship, your emotions safe will unlock. That means that you will have access to the love that you need to help your husband, but other feelings will spill out, too. As a result, you will also feel waves of anger, sadness, and/or anxiety. How intense those feelings are depends on how much you have locked up your feelings and for how long. If you are not one to lock up any feelings, then you won't need to deal with this at all. If you have locked up everything, you may need some extra counseling help to deal with your feelings before you can work on the skills in this book. The good news is that feelings of love return strongly after the problems are taken care of. It will be the wonderful reward for your efforts.

Your Husband May Have Shut Down His Love

Do you remember I said that your husband may be reacting to pain that is not coming from you? It could be coming from work, for example, or from problems with other family members. Pain is pain. This means that if your husband is overwhelmed with issues not related to you, he may have shut down his feelings in order to deal with them. This means that he will also have shut down his love toward you. You may be sensing that he loves you less and if you told him so, he may well agree with you. But, once his problems are dealt with or he deals with them in another way that doesn't turn off his feelings, his love for you will spring back to life. Not that it was dead, it was locked out of reach in his emotional safe.

You may also witness his angry moods, depression, or anxiety in response to another situation. Although when he is with you, he is not in that situation, mentally he may still be dealing with it. Men generally have a pretty good ability to compartmentalize their life—to deal with each area of their life as though it were in a completely separate box. But, when the stress is intense, things spill over between boxes.

How Women Get Stuck

Sometimes, our way of dealing with emotional pain prevents us from getting the help we need to fix things in a positive way. With our emotions dulled, we feel more like we have everything under control. Or with our anger cranked up, we become insistent that the only solution is for our partner to change. Or for us to change partners. When our emotions are intense, recommendations to get counseling or coaching bring the dread of dealing with all these feelings again. There is a sort of paradox here. Do nothing and you may be able to keep your emotions under control, although your relationship will continue to suffer. Get professional help and the pain may come back full force as you open up about your problems.

It's a choice between feeling intense pain and letting things get worse. It's no wonder that many women don't make a choice at all, letting years go by.

To use a physical, rather than an emotional example, if a bone is broken, it will heal in whatever position it is kept in, even if it is misaligned. Such a misalignment would cause some level of pain and disability for the rest of a person's life. To heal properly, it would need to be broken again, aligned correctly, and re-healed. Though everyone would like to have correctly aligned bones, no one likes the thought of re-breaking one of their bones to do it. This is similar to many people who have learned to deal with the pain of their relationship, though they are still unhappy. When they think about working on it, with or without professional help, they know there is going to be a very tough period to go through. If you are at that point, I can't tell you there is an easy solution. But, I can tell you that this intense pain will only be temporary and that you won't regret it later.

I also want to encourage you to see this as a possible explanation for your husband's lack of desire to work on your relationship. Men are very brave outwardly, but internally they are often afraid to reopen emotional wounds, especially since so few men know how to deal with strong emotions. They are afraid not only of the hurt they could receive, but also of the hurt they could give in getting things out in the open. Men are physically powerful and have learned to control themselves much more than they have learned to let things out. What comes naturally, though painfully, to you may be unthinkable for your husband.

When You Don't Feel Like Working on the Relationship

We are naturally not at our best when we are under attack, being rejected, or ignored. At times like these the last thing we feel like doing is helping the person who is attacking, rejecting, or ignoring us. That is alright. We are human beings after all, so being tempted to reject or get revenge on our partners should not disturb us.

Temptations are not the same as actions. Knowing this helps us to accept our own feelings and those of our partners. Because they are human, too.

However, we do need to have a way to get back on track. Our natural emotional responses sure are not going to build the relationship. And they are not going to help your husband to change. But, change must happen if your relationship is going to get better.

If You Don't Know What to Do

Of course most people realize that attacking, defending, and avoiding are not healthy ways to resolve problems even if they feel like doing that. Unfortunately, few of us receive any direct training in how to do any better. Even so, we have learned something about managing conflict from our parents, from television, and from our other relationships. In our past we may not have always gotten along with others, but most of the time, we have been able to patch things up. Whatever we have learned to do in the past, we will do again. There are two reasons for this: 1) people continue to do what works, even if it only works a little, and 2) because our ways always make sense to us. In fact, our thinking always makes so much sense to us, we are amazed to find our partners think differently! "What is wrong with him?" you may wonder.

Because our thinking makes so much sense to us, we first try to help our partners to understand our reasoning. I believe this is actually a good place to start. Many times problems are caused by misunderstandings and miscommunications. You and your partner may have problems because of misunderstanding and not because you actually believe different things. This is also true when you have a difficult husband, but the problem may come when you try to talk with him. His emotions or yours may trigger behaviors that prevent good communication. You two may not be able to communicate well enough to realize you are in agreement!

So there is the actual problem, and there is an inability to communicate about the problem, which is another problem. For this reason, many women stop talking to their husbands about problems.

10

Not because of a natural desire to attack or defend, but mainly as a reaction to avoid more problems. If that is what you are doing, I'm going to let you off the hook about that (whew, you thought I was going to say something different, didn't you?). You should *not* try to talk about problems with your husband if it just causes more problems. But, you do need to learn to communicate effectively with him. A relationship without communication is like popcorn without butter.

When attempts to communicate don't work, and before they give up, women usually either repeatedly try to communicate in ineffective ways, or they turn to one of three standby methods for dealing with conflict. I believe these three standby "conflict solvers" don't solve conflict at all, but that they actually maintain conflict or create new conflicts. They do, however, reduce stress to a manageable level. These three methods are compromise, distance, and silence. It won't surprise you that distance and silence do nothing to fix a problem and certainly don't build a relationship. But the *harm* done by compromise is easier not to notice.

Beware of Too Many Compromises

Compromise makes you feel like things are getting better because you get something of what you want while your husband gets something of what he wants. If that was all there was to compromise, I would agree that it's great. But, the other side of compromise is that you lose something that you want and your partner loses something that he wants. It is a zero gain solution. Rather than a win-win solution, compromise is a don't lose-don't lose solution. Zero gain solutions help people get along peacefully, but they don't help them get closer.

Regular compromise is great for society but disaster for couples. A little compromise here and there, like a little fast food, probably will grease the wheels and be an easy way to squeeze through a tight spot. But, a continuous use of compromise is like a continuous diet of fast food. Even if it were free, it would be undesirable, because the results would create too much of what you don't want. People can only compromise so long before they feel like they have lost too much.

How much compromise is too much? Let's compare this to the same question about shouting. If a couple often shouts at each other, their focus will be on that, because that is where their pain is most keenly felt. Learning how often they have shouting matches though, would not tell me as much about their relationship as how often they tell each other they love each other, or how close they feel most of the time. If they more often feel close than they shout, they're probably doing ok. There is no specific rule about how often a couple can or can't shout at each other and still have a good relationship. The same is true for compromise. How often you compromise is not nearly as important as how often you help each other to get what you really want. Whereas compromise takes something away, helping adds something. Couples who give a lot to each other may need to compromise often, but with little damage. Couples who give little or nothing at all will make their relationship worse with every compromise they make. They will grow more and more resentful at what they *have to* give up. As you learn to help your husband get what he wants and he to help you get what you want, the compromises will be less important. And, you will both become more eager to please each other instead of trying to protect what little you have. You will move from a zero gain solution to a win-win solution.

The Problem With Patience

What happens when someone has been using silence, distance, or compromise for a long time—for example, a number of years? The more time that passes, the more people feel cheated, robbed of their lifetime. As time passes they see their appearance changing in the mirror; their friends and coworkers achieving things that they haven't. They begin to feel like they have given too much and gotten too little in return. They start to resent their partners. Resentment is a feeling we have towards others, but it is always created by our own decisions. Like the decision to give up something that was important to us and later miss. Like the decision to wait and wait and wait when we need to take action.

Some women have given up children, rather than bring them into a bad marriage. Others have given up careers, or paid their husband's way through college only to be divorced after graduation. Some have given years of care and attention to someone who gave them almost nothing in return. Working or loving for scraps would make anyone resentful.

I'm not trying to convince you to leave your partner—far from it. I am trying to convince you that compromise, silence, distance, and even patient endurance are not your friends nor your husband's. Use them outside your home, prudently, to get along with difficult people, but don't use them inside your home to get along with your difficult husband. You need to do more than just keep the peace if you want to have a good relationship. And so does he. Learn more effective methods for dealing with him so that he can learn more effectively to love you. Then you will both have what you want.

What about the Recommendation to Give "Unconditional Love"?

I get frustrated by well meaning pastoral counselors who recommend women to love their husbands unconditionally, but then stop there. I agree wholeheartedly that we need to love as much as we can—unconditionally, if possible. But, we need to be very sure that what we are doing is actually loving. Love does what is in the best interest of the other person—*even if they don't like it*. So, a mother or father will punish a young child who tries to run into the road, and doesn't give her candy for dinner no matter how big a tantrum she has. A girl walks away from her boyfriend when he calls her an ugly name. And a wife sets limits on her husband's harmful behavior. This is a big part of what love is about. No woman who endures her husband's mistreatment is really doing him any favors.

But, Isn't Love Supposed to Be Patient?

When we love someone, we don't let them do harmful things to us because it hurts them as well as us. If your son is being mean to your daughter, you stop him for your daughter's sake as well as your son's. Teaching your daughter just to be "patient" in this situation would not prepare her well for her future. It is important for her to have healthy boundaries and respect herself. And, your son needs to learn to respect women—something vital for his future relationships.

Patience is about continually doing the right thing, without giving up, and not about continually enduring the wrong thing. And patience is also the decision not to return evil for evil (even when our partner deserves it). It's not revenge when we teach our partners not to hurt us. It is love because it helps them have a better relationship with us. It is putting the relationship first. It is honoring our partner and our commitment.

Changing Your Focus

An understanding of what love really is brings us to the proper place to focus our attention for solving ongoing problems. Instead of focusing on the question, "How can I get my husband to stop doing this?" we will focus on "How can I help my husband change, for his sake and my own?" If there was no way to do that, then I would join the throngs of free advice givers on the internet who just say, "Dump him, who needs a man like that?" They see your problem, but fail to see the human being you are married to. They fail to see what you, and he, would lose if you can work things out but don't. Being committed means doing *all* that we can to make a good relationship.

Facing the Fear of Rejection

We run the risk of rejection even when we do the right things, and sometimes especially when we do. But to allow more and more harm to come to our relationships for fear of rejection seems like an altogether more foolish and less loving thing to do. And, if we do happen to be rejected in the midst of our loving choices and healthy boundaries, we still leave the door open for change. When you do what's right, though the relationship end with sadness, it would not end with regret. No one regrets doing their best, even when things don't turn out so well.

Helping your husband to change will mean putting the relationship first. A healthy and happy long term relationship will be the star that you steer by, and not your feelings at the moment, nor your husband's. It will be a guide to better choices and a hope that you can hold on to. In the light of a good long-term relationship, attacking, defending, distancing, and unchanging endurance are all revealed to be ugly. They are the relationship destroyers. Healthy boundaries, and firm-but-loving guidance, are revealed to be the marks of true commitment to the relationship.

The Road Ahead

Your husband loves you. With the interventions in this book you will learn to help him love you better. It is what he wants to do, despite all outward appearances. His harmful behaviors have been hurting him even longer than they have been hurting you. And if you leave him, those behaviors will just go on hurting him and yet another woman. For you, helping him will be a thankless job. But only at first. The more you teach him to love you, the closer both of you will become. Let's be clear that by "teaching," I don't mean sitting him down like a student and explaining things to him while he takes notes. If you had a man like that, you would have an easy one and not a difficult one! You teach simply by changing what you say and do. When he adjusts to your changes, he will have "learned." With men, actions always teach better than words.

Some women, when they start relationship coaching, ask me how they can change their husband's personality. They want to be assured that they aren't just teaching their husbands how to love them better, but how to love others better as well (with other family members, for example). To this, I say your husband will do with others what he learns from you, to the extent that it works better with others. Old habits will continue in old relationships, but you will see the "new" him more and more with new relationships.

Be concerned with your relationship with him and your own relationship with others. God does as much, and I don't think we can do better than that.

2

GETTING READY TO MAKE POSITIVE CHANGES

Do you have a difficult relationship? You hardly need my help to figure out whether you have a difficult relationship. Like pornography, it's hard to define, but you know it when you see it. Or, in the case of a difficult relationship, you know it when you feel it. There's always too much of what you don't want and too little of what you do. The feelings are either too intense and too bad or the feelings are just not there at all.

It's when the feelings are not there at all that things are at their worst. If you are going to do anything, you need to do it before it gets to that point, because once you are there—once you have burned out on your relationship—it can still be saved, but you won't *care* enough to save it. Burnout, the lack of emotions that comes from emotional fatigue, accounts for the end of more relationships than strong feelings do.

If you are nearing the burnout point, you need to regroup and recharge before you work on your relationship. If you don't feel much like working on your relationship, you will probably admit that you could use a good recharge. Wouldn't it be nice if you could just plug into a recharger like you do with your cell phone? Until that technology comes out, you will need to use old fashioned methods.

Recovering from Emotional Burnout

The best way to start recharging is to stop doing those things that are burning you out. No matter how much you feel like you're effectively dealing with your husband, take a look in the mirror and check your emotional pulse. If your reflection is not looking any happier and your feelings make you wonder if the relationship is dead or dying, you're *not* dealing with your husband effectively. *You* are surviving, but your relationship is not. Your emotional survival is important though, so give yourself credit for that. Many women have done worse.

Although your response to your husband is not very effective, I will agree with you that your husband's behavior is causing the problems. Like a firefighter, you didn't cause the fire, but you do need to have an effective way to put it out. Burning out doesn't mean your situation can't be helped. It just means that you are overusing ineffective methods like complaining, explaining, or avoiding. This is like trying to put out a three alarm fire with a garden hose. The way you are dealing with your husband probably does work a little, or else you wouldn't be doing it. When something works just a little, we are tempted to do more of it (for example, because avoiding talking about sensitive topics does reduce conflict, some people don't talk at all). When what you are doing creates distance, the more you do it, the more distant your relationship will become. To become closer, you will need to exchange low effectiveness methods for highly effective ones. You need to put down the garden hose and call 911. The more you take effective actions, the sooner the problems will stop and the closer you will become.

Providing you with new and effective methods is what this book is all about. Keep reading, keep an open mind, and keep a finger on your relationship pulse. When the things in this book sound like they are just too tough or wouldn't work, your fading love pulse will remind you that a new approach is needed. Getting real about what will happen to your relationship without a new approach will help you to keep an open mind. Let's try that right now for practice. Please respond to the following sentence:

If I don't find a different way to deal with my husband, this is what is going to happen to my relationship: _____ .

You need to keep asking yourself this same question because it supports change and change is hard. But once the changes are made, once the fire is out, life will be a whole lot easier.

Difficult Relationships Have Too Much of This and Too Little of That

A difficult relationship has an excess of things that push a couple apart. The chief troublemakers are resentment, selfishness, jealousy, insecurity, intolerance, and the failure to see one's partner as a whole person. Ever get the feeling that your husband doesn't really know you or doesn't understand what you really want? It's very possible that he has only taken the time to know those parts of you which relate to himself. The parts that he can see. But there is a lot more to you than that! You had interests and dreams for the future even before he came along, and you still do. If he is jealous, insecure, or selfish, it will be hard for him to accept parts of you that don't require him. A difficult man won't be motivated to help you succeed if it means you could get along without him. And with a difficult man you will find yourself being careful of what you say. You may even give up friends and activities that make your life more meaningful.

Interventions which remove harmful excesses, like extreme carefulness, will tear down the wall between you two and will show him that he is not at the center of the universe. He will see you in a new, different, and more complete way. It will take him a little time to get used to the new you. If you haven't learned how to stand firmly on your own two feet, it may take time for you to get used to the new you, too.

A difficult relationship also has a lack of things that draw people together. The most sorely needed qualities are love, acceptance, cooperation, respect, and security. I'm sure you would like to see these things in place before you start helping your husband to change. Unfortunately, you can only get an increase in these things as a *result* of your changes. Think of it this way—if he already had a good supply of these qualities, you wouldn't need him to change. You wouldn't want him to change. You would want him not to change! So, the idea that your husband needs to treat you better before he gets any help from you will put you in a bind. You will be waiting for him to change before you help him to change. That's deadlock. That's stuck-ness. Helping him when he is not helping you is not fair, but it is necessary if you want to improve your relationship

Stop Playing the Blame Game

Women with difficult husbands often get to the point where they resent having to do anything for them. Resentment is created when we blame someone else for the choices that we are making. It goes along with this kind of thought—"It's not fair. *I have to* do this for him, although he doesn't …" This kind of thinking is actually an excess on your part. The thinking, not the activity, makes you feel like a victim. It makes you feel obligated and slave-like. And it makes you angry. A small change in thinking can free you from these feelings.

You can start to decrease your resentment by seeing it like it *really* is. You don't *have to* do any of those things for him. In fact, you could leave him tomorrow. But, you *choose* to do those things because you don't know how to deal with him if you don't, or because it would be too much of a hassle to stop, or because you worry about how he would react. You are choosing to do those things because it is easier or because you don't know what else to do. Taking responsibility by seeing your actions as your choices, will increase your personal power, make you feel less like a victim, and suggest to you that you can choose to do things in other ways. You have the power and freedom to choose how you want to live.

If you want to blame your husband for *his* behavior, go ahead. It's where the blame belongs. But, start to take responsibility for your own behavior. It will decrease your resentment and that will help your relationship. Notice that I *didn't* say stop doing those things which help your husband. That will just stir up the hornet's nest and cause more problems. But, take responsibility for them. See them as something you are choosing to do. You are choosing to help him. After you help him to change, you will be glad to do those things for him. Your misery, your resentment, is connected to your inability to deal with him effectively. The more effective you become, the less of a threat or burden he will be, the more you will love him, and the less you will resent doing things for him.

Taking Away Your Husband's Emotional Remote Control

There is something that bothers people more than a lie—it's the truth. If someone says you are a two headed zombie, it won't bother you because it is ridiculous. Most completely untrue things are. If someone says you are selfish, it will bother you because it is partly true. You are at least partly concerned about yourself. Whether your husband is anxious, angry, or depressed, he undoubtedly will say things to you or about you which are partly true and therefore will upset you. All he has to do is say those things and it is just like pressing an emotional remote control connected to your head. Which means who has the power over your emotions? He does. Who gives it to him? You do. Every true thing about ourselves, that we don't like, creates an emotional "button" that others can push.

To short-circuit his remote control, you will need to decrease another relationship excess—defensiveness. Defensiveness is what people use to "protect" themselves emotionally, from the truth. Start to listen for the *truth* in what your husband says when he is pushing your buttons. And then, shamelessly agree with it. For example, if your husband says, "You don't love me," admit that sometimes you don't. But leave it at that. Don't launch into an explanation or accusations. Or another example, "You don't care about anyone except yourself," (often said by selfish husbands). Admit to him that you do want to take good care of yourself. "I do want to take good care of myself." If you can learn to do this, no one will be able to push your buttons again. It's only when you resist, deny, explain, or counterattack that they know they have got you. The truth will set you free to be successful with the interventions in this book. Because if all he has to do is say a half truth to make you emotionally lose it, you won't be able to make changes. His verbal jabs (whether whispered, cried, or shouted) are his way to keep you at an emotionally safe distance. One that he is comfortable with. Learn to deal with the jabs, and you will be able to use the step by step methods in this book to help him change. Be tough now, so you can have tenderness later. Do that and he can be, once again, the man you have waited your whole life for.

Earn His Respect

Lack of respect is one of the most common relationship destroyers among both men and women. One of the principle ways that you will make your relationship better with your difficult husband is to *earn* his respect. Respect, like trust, is earned and cannot be given until it is earned. Is there anything your husband could say that would make you respect him if he still continued bad behaviors? Or would he have to change what he did as well as what he said before you would respect him? His making changes would mean a whole lot more than just telling you, wouldn't it? In the same way, saying "believe me" repeatedly does not create trust. But consistently telling the truth does. It works the same way for both men and women. Saying, "I'm not going to tolerate that behavior," will earn you *no* respect if you then tolerate it. In fact, if you say something and then don't do it, you will be respected even less than before. People build respect only when they walk like they talk. That's one major reason you should never threaten to do something. If you don't follow through, you lose respect and the problems become even worse. If you are in a public place with your husband and he is treating you badly, and you tell him, "You do that one more time and I'm leaving," what does that teach? It teaches him that it's ok for him to mistreat you until he is warned. It teaches him you will tolerate a certain amount of mistreatment. A woman who walks out the *first* time a man mistreats her gets respect fast. You would respect such a woman too, wouldn't you? You don't need to be aggressive to get respect. A very gentle person can get respect. What is required is consistency between words and behavior.

The work that you will do as a result of following the methods in this book will get you more respect. That's important because your husband is not going to be able to love you better if he can't respect you. Respect and love go hand in hand. We will use methods which build respect in a positive way.

Lowering His Resistance To Your Changes

If you value your relationship and believe that your relationship should be positive, you must talk positively and behave positively. This doesn't mean being happy or cheerful all the time. It means doing what you want your husband to do—put your relationship first. That's not easy to do when you're upset and it's not easy for him either. But you can learn to do it. You can give your husband the message that your relationship with him is very important for you and you won't participate in damaging it. This consistent message will set the stage for your being able to disagree with him (without arguing or fighting) and for doing things differently than he wants you to. We want him to know why you are doing what you are doing. So, just doing things differently won't be enough— explanations are required. Your husband will need to have a basic understanding of why you are making changes. How you say this is very important, so I will help you know just what to say. In the process, I will help you to learn and use constructive communication.

In applying the methods in this book, you will learn to do what is best for your relationship. Your husband is welcome to challenge it, especially if he has a way that is even better (you are open to him talking about ways to improve the relationship, right?). None of the methods you will learn are secret things that you will do behind your husband's back. On the contrary—they will be right out in front.

They will earn you respect, and invite him to come up with even better ways if he doesn't like yours. It is a win-win situation.

Stop Being Codependent

Respect is lost in relationships mainly when we say that we value the relationship, but then do things that harm the relationship or assist our partners in doing something which harms the relationship (known as codependence). If a man repeatedly abuses a woman, who is lacking in respect? Both of them. The husband damages the relationship by abusing his wife, whether physically or emotionally, and whether by violence, verbal abuse, or neglect. The wife also loses her husband's respect by allowing this to go on—by continuing to participate in it. Certainly she isn't helping her husband by allowing him to do things which harm her, the relationship, and himself. This bears repeating—you can't show love to your husband, or earn his respect, by allowing him to do things which harm himself, you, or the relationship.

Everything that your husband does to harm you or to harm the relationship also harms himself. Letting such behaviors go on deprives him of what he could have, with you, if he didn't do such behaviors. It reduces his respect for you. And unless he is an insensitive man, he loses respect for himself. We don't have to think of a wildly dangerous man to imagine this situation. Even a man who would rather spend his time with his computer than with his wife is harming his relationship. It is neglect, at least. He will not feel like a better husband for it. Can you imagine him thinking, "I'm a good husband because I spend all my time on the computer (gambling, golfing, at work, etc.)"?

Reduce Conflict

Difficult relationships may have too much conflict. Conflict is not necessarily fighting. Even two people who never talk to each other can have conflict. You can *feel* conflict. Conflict is the result of two people who want things that are mutually incompatible. I want to watch channel 7 and you want to watch channel 12. I want to talk and you want silence. I want you to leave me alone and you want to be closer to me. Ironically, couples have a lot of conflict, trying to get closer, even though the conflict just drives them further apart. The closeness they desire is the same, but the methods they use are not compatible with being close. For example, fighting about distance just creates more distance.

When a husband and wife no longer desire to be close, conflict drops off. That's because both their actions and desires are in agreement at that point! Neither wants to be close and each does his own thing without interference. Any time you show me an intact, high conflict relationship, I will show you two people who desperately want to have a close relationship but don't know how. If you have a high conflict relationship (whether you are fighting or not), and your husband is not trying to end it, it means he also wants to have a better relationship with you, but he doesn't know how. And neither do you. The great news is you can learn to make changes that will help him to make changes. All the energy that has been going into conflict can then go into joining, sharing, helping, and loving.

Increase Acceptance

Lack of acceptance happens when we fail to see our partners for who they really are. Acceptance is different from agreement. I accept that skunks spray stinky stuff when they are scared. If I don't, I might get pretty stinky when I come across one. Whether I like it or not, does not matter. That's just the way skunks are. I accept that vinegar is sour. I am not going to repeatedly put vinegar on my pancakes and get angry because it is not sweet. There are many things about our partners that are not going to change. These may be physical features, intelligence, their relatives, their need to take care of your stepchildren, or many other things. Seeing these things clearly, not holding them against your partner, and making room for them in your life are what acceptance is about. You have things to accept about your husband, and he has things to accept about you.

Acceptance happens in stages. The first stage is denial, when there is no acceptance. This is a "skunks smell nice, vinegar is sweet," kind of blindness. You can see this when your husband is trying to change something about you that is not changeable. This is when he will have the most anger and frustration about it. Many men, for example, get frustrated with their wife's need to socialize with other people besides them. Women are social creatures. Trying to change that is like trying to grow a sunflower in a dark basement. The harder he tries, the more harm will result. Women too, are often in denial about their husband's inability to be changed by words alone.

Acceptance begins to happen when we stop trying to change something about our partner. At that point we become more sad and less angry. When you don't change in a way that your husband wants you to, he will eventually realize that you are just not going to be the way he wants you to be (locked in a cage, under control, only attending to him, a supermodel, etc.). It is a real experience of loss for him. He loses his image of how he believed you were or could be. It's kind of pitiable, but it's necessary if he is to love who you really are.

The last stage of acceptance is adjustment and accommodation. When this happens, he will no longer be focused on changing you nor moaning, complaining, or sulking about it. He will be working around it or in spite of it. It won't be an area of conflict between the two of you. That's why working to get him to accept certain realities will lead to reduced conflict and help both of you to get on with loving each other—*as you really are.* And that's how people want to be loved. All of the techniques in this book build acceptance so that the two of you can become closer.

As you may know, many young people make a commitment to their partners before accepting realities about how their partners are. They are still hoping their partners will change something they don't like. This usually doesn't happen. This means the difficult process of acceptance happens after they have already made a commitment.

One of the reasons the first few years of marriage can be so difficult is because of the number of differences that have to be accepted.

Lack of acceptance happens most to people who think there is only one right way, so that both people must do and think the same thing, or else one person is wrong. People who have a hard time accepting others differences are often angry. But few people would do well with a partner who was identical to herself (or himself). In reality it is the diversity in relationships that make them strong. For example, if he is strong where you are weak, that helps you with things that are difficult for you. If you are more social, you can help him to connect to others in ways he couldn't by himself. You are attracted to the best of qualities in men, and he in women. It's the best parts of each other which brought you two together and only the worst parts that push you both apart. Acceptance comes when we see both the good and the bad, love anyhow, and persist in using the best parts of ourselves to build the relationship. It also means each partner needs boundaries to deal with their own and their partner's bad parts that may harm the relationship. There is no person on earth without such bad parts. Having better boundaries, not finding a better partner, is the key to a better relationship. We can except that fire burns, but we don't have to let it burn down our house. Distinguishing between what you don't like and what is actually harmful to the relationship is an important distinction which will help you to know what needs to be accepted and when you need to have good boundaries. You also must distinguish between what he doesn't like and what you do that is bad for the relationship. Even a difficult husband is sometimes right.

One of the most helpful things you can do for your relationship is to see your husband as a caterpillar and to help him to see you as the same. With the right care, your natural tendencies and desires will, over time, turn each of you into a butterfly. You need to support each other's differences, when they are not harmful to your relationship. As a woman dealing with a difficult man, you will also need to be able to assert your own differences, when they are not harmful to the relationship. Too many women *stop themselves* from becoming beautiful butterflies. If you do that, it will deprive your husband as well as yourself. Waking up next to a partner who is growing in life, love, and happiness keeps a relationship fresh.

End Control Issues

There is no one who can hang onto their relationship by force, but there are an abundance of people who try. The more we fear, the tighter we grasp, and the more we lose our grip. Your husband grew up with a lot of cultural rules and experiences. He chooses his actions according to what he knows (his habits) and according to what he fears (his insecurities). You can be *his* butterfly, but only if he doesn't cage you in a glass jar. Love is given freely, not taken by force. Knowing each other intimately, trusting, growing, supporting, and feeling free are all part of the same package. You can have that. And as much as you want it, he wants it too (for himself, at least). Keeping that in mind will be key to his loosening his grip on you.

The more your husband restricts you and controls you, the less freedom he can have for himself. If he wants you to stay home all the time rather than spend time with your friends, then you can give him what he wants. Tell him you will be happy to be with him instead of your friends. The only condition is that he spend that time with you, doing something meaningful. If he doesn't follow through, go out with your friends. Most men will decide very soon that it's ok for you to go out once in awhile. Then, that will be what they want, too. The more control you give your husband, the more he will resist it. If your husband is always telling you what to do, don't fight it. Instead, nicely ask for his advice with *everything*, and he will tire of giving you advice and stop telling you what to do. There are other methods to use for over-controlling men, but this works most of the time, is low conflict, and promotes acceptance. A change on your part brings change on his part.

Sometimes wives try to reign in or control their husbands. That happens when they *fear* what their husbands might do. For example, they fear that their husband might leave them for someone else, so they try to closely monitor what he does. When she finds out that he is not cheating on her or heading into the danger zone, she feels relieved. Her relief rewards and maintains these actions. Her husband, though, is not rewarded. Instead, he feels that he must be secretive or careful about what he is doing, lest his wife should make something out of it or try to restrict his activities. He starts to look over his shoulder before he talks to a woman. Then, his carefulness gets mistaken for deceptiveness.

If this is hard to imagine, just reverse husband and wife in the previous example. The husband wants to know when and where his wife is going all the time, so he can be sure that she is not seeing anyone else or even going near other men. He feels relieved when he gets information about her comings and goings, but she feels controlled. This particular instance of insecurity is jealousy. Whether it is jealousy or some other insecurity, our insecurities push our partners further away. The more we push our partners away, the more distant they become from us, and the more likely they will actually do what we fear. In this way people make their fears come true.

Overcome Your Fears

This is the point about insecurities—we create with our behaviors whatever we fear. If we fear cheating, our behaviors actually push our partners further in that direction. If you fear your husband's anger, then you will be all the more timid about it and seek to avoid it rather than deal with it. That makes it all the more likely that he will use anger against you. His anger is more effective when you fear it. People spend more time and energy trying to avoid things they are insecure about than they would dealing with what they fear. The fear of failure stops more relationships, more businesses, and more goals from being achieved than any other obstacle. It is the fear of failure that prevents success. Fortunately, when you learn how to deal with what you fear, you no longer need your fears. That means that simply by learning to deal with something, you are also making it less likely to happen.

With this book, you can learn to deal with many of your fears simply by learning how to deal with whatever you are trying to avoid or prevent. You will learn to deal with anger when it happens. Then you don't need to fear it happening. You will also learn to deal with cheating and lying. You will also learn how to deal with a hurt or wounded husband. Sometimes we can be so afraid of hurting someone that we don't do what we need to do to help them. A good intervention may make your husband feel hurt emotionally, but when your motivation is out of love, you don't need to fear it. Like taking a sliver out of a finger, that little pain may prevent a worse infection.

Let Go of Guilt

Difficult relationships stimulate fantasies about the relationship ending or about finding someone else. Some of these fantasies can really bother us and not at all match our values. It is kind of the mind's way of seeking escape or seeking something that we need. More tolerable fantasies come in the form of "if only," such as "If only I didn't marry him." These are kind of magical, "undoing" thoughts. Fantasies about the past are more tolerable to most people because they are impossible. Unfortunately, these "if only" kinds of thoughts also create emotional distance. Although these fantasies *are not* signs that something is wrong with you or that you need medication, they *are* a sign that relationship intervention is needed. You can either distance yourself from your husband with such thinking, or you can work on the relationship so that such thinking is unnecessary. This is the choice point that comes in every difficult relationship. Take action, or not. You may not succeed with your intervention, but you will regret it if you don't try. If you don't make a choice at all, these thoughts, and the emotional distance that goes with them, will happen automatically. No matter how bad something seems, there is no problem that someone hasn't found a way to deal with positively. It's your job to find and use these positive ways rather than feel guilty with secret desires.

Summary

If you have seen something of yourself or your husband in this chapter, I hope it *comforts* you to know these things are normal and *disturbs* you enough to be intent on changing things. Your husband is not a monster and you need to make sure that you don't see him as one. Seeing him as the enemy may help you to justify your feelings, but you don't need to justify your feelings. You are a human being and your feelings are your feelings. To save your marriage, you must think about loving two people—your husband and yourself. You must see that you were a little girl, who has grown up into the woman you are now; who needs to grow more to be able to deal with things her childhood didn't prepare her for. Like the way your husband is now. And, you need to see that your husband has grown from a young boy, doing the best that he could, but who needs your help to continue to grow. You can do that by not being codependent for his harmful behaviors. For his sake? No. For the both of you and for your children, too.

When you help your husband to change, you will be loving both him and yourself, and you will be putting the relationship first. The blind cannot lead the blind. It is up to the one who can see to lead. For now, I am the one who can see how to make changes and I must lead you. Later, you will be the one to see and you must lead your husband. When he is able to see, and change, you will both be able to walk side by side. That is the goal of this book and hopefully your goal, too.

"I married the first man I ever kissed. When I tell this to my children, they just about throw up." Barbara Bush

3

MAKING GOOD CHOICES WHEN YOU HAVE A DIFFICULT HUSBAND OR PARTNER

So, you have a difficult relationship because you have a difficult husband, right? If he couldn't change, then you would have little choice except to leave him or put up with the way he is. Maybe you have been putting up with him because you thought change wasn't possible. And, perhaps you are even contemplating leaving him now because you have been putting up with him too long. Fortunately, unless your husband was the same when you married him as he is now, he is not likely to have an unchangeable personality problem (even if he is the same, change is still possible). The changes your husband has made since you met him are most likely habits, or emotional coping styles, or both. Habits can change. The way we cope can and does change as a result of experience (if you sucked your thumb as a child, you probably don't now). And, we can continue to learn to more effectively deal with things that emotionally stress us. Because of all these possibilities, your husband can change, and you can change. Positive change is called growth. How the rest of your relationship will go has not been written. The choices you make and the options you choose will influence what happens. This is your greatest power.

Ignoring the Vocal Minority

Before I get into what your options are, I want to warn you about two groups of people. They have an agenda, and they have a rhetoric, propaganda to make you give up on your relationship. One group is the "men haters," and one group is the "badly wounded." Some people belong to both groups. Because of their experiences with men and because of what they have learned about men, they believe the best way to deal with a difficult husband is to get rid of him. They will tell you many horror stories about themselves and others. But, they won't tell you about the even greater number of women who have improved their relationships with difficult men. They have an emotionally vested interest in not learning that they, too, could have improved their relationship. No one who has divorced wants to think they could have saved their relationship. Doubtless, this book will be greatly criticized by them. They are not bad people, but they are misinformed and injured. They will try to protect you by telling you to end your relationship or to take drastic action to make your husband put his tail between his legs.

The facts are that almost everyone who has had a relationship has had relationship problems. This goes for all kinds of relationships—father, mother, sister, brother, child, friend, boyfriend, girlfriend, and spouse. In the majority of cases, these relationship problems are overcome. Most kids who fight with their parents later have a good relationship with them. And many people who break up, get together again. There are far more temporary separations than there are divorces, And some people who divorce remarry the same person. While many marriages have been destroyed by conflict and coldness, even more couples have overcome conflict and become close. So, your first choice is whether to listen to the naysayers and give up before you even try *effective* measures (I'm sure you have been trying something). It's an important choice. Some women want to somehow decide both ways and half try, or make a half-hearted try. That simply will not work. Either do or don't do. To half-try is to not do. There is nothing that can be accomplished in this world by a half try. Don't believe me? Go ahead, half try to write your name, or half try to turn on the light, or half try to talk to your husband. A half try never gets the job done. Women who "half try" know they didn't really try at all.

What If It Doesn't Work?

But, what if you try (really try) and it doesn't work? Isn't there still time to end the relationship if you want to? For some reason, naysayers always want people to take drastic action "now!", "before it's too late." Too late for what? I agree that waiting won't change your situation, but I think it's better to try fixing up the house before you decide to tear it down. You just might like the result. And it will save you a lot of regret if you could have done something about it and you didn't. Choosing to do all that you can do now will mean no regrets later.

The Psychology of Change

If you're still reading this far, then there is still something inside you that wants things to work out. They can. And I will show you how to work them out. First, though, you will need to learn some basic psychology about why people change, and why they don't. Understanding this will make you more effective in changing your husband, and your reactions to him, for the better.

The fact is, some people remain remarkably stable in their personalities and behavior from the time they are young children until they grow old and die. Others, though, change a lot from childhood to adulthood. The most common reason people change is because their experiences change. Their parents divorce, they move from the country to the city (or vice versa), they are in a war, someone close to them dies, they break up with a loved one, they become poor or rich, get an education, or drop out of school. Looking back at your own history, you can probably see how you changed and figure out what happened to change you. If you know people from your childhood who have changed very little, then it is likely they still live in the same town where they grew up and the demands on them have not changed much.

To "change" means to adapt—to match the emotional and physical demands put on us. Once we adapt, we maintain our behavior through habit until that habit no longer works. If you and your husband have been behaving the same way toward each other for the past three months, you are both following a habit—the way you have adapted to each other.

Heredity also plays a part in what we do. But generally, regardless of someone's genes, he will not walk in front of a bus. He will still put his pants on one leg at a time. And he will go to work and do what the boss says so that the paychecks will keep coming and there is food to put in the refrigerator. Heredity gives way to necessity. That is how our species has survived. Keeping these things in mind will help you to remember that regardless of your husband's particular personality, birth sign, or the problems that run in his family, he still has learned to adapt to his environment in order to survive. In fact, he adapted well enough to attract you, and keep you (at least so far). If he were purely a product of his genetics, he would not have been able to attract you. He learned to date girls (especially ones like you) and he is doing now what he knows how to do to have a relationship with you. And, although your relationship may not be good for either of you right now, it is working a little. Husbands, like most everyone else, continue to do what works a little. Difficult men are like people who drive a clunky car, belching blue smoke. As long as it works, they are ok. When it breaks down, then they fix it. There will be no significant demand on your husband to adapt—to change for the better—until his way breaks down.

The fact that your husband has changed since the beginning of your relationship is evidence that he has the ability to change. He is difficult because of the habits he now has, and not because he is somehow a different person than the one you married. He is a "difficult man" only to the extent that you don't know how to deal with his bothersome behaviors. If you knew how to deal with them, he would not be difficult for you. The behavior problem is his, learning how to deal with those behaviors (rather than tolerating, being codependent for, or avoiding them) is yours. And why would you want to learn? Because, just as your husband had the potential to change to how he is now, he has the same potential to be better than he is now. To adapt in the positive direction. Which means your relationship can be better. In fact, you can be closer to your husband than you have ever been before. When you are done making changes, to which he must adapt, from his perspective he will have made a great achievement in learning to deal with you! And, he will not go back to the way he is now as long as you don't. So, although you won't get applause, you will get change and a relationship you enjoy more. And that's what you're after, right?

What You Believe Makes All the Difference

As we can see, it's your belief about whether your husband can change and your knowledge about how to help him that will make the ultimate difference. Your head must be screwed on straight before you can screw his on straight. Believing that your husband is corrupt, defective, personality disordered, or unredeemable would lead to the fall of your relationship as much as his behavior would.

Knowing how to stop your husband's bad behavior toward you and how to create changes that help both him and you will save your relationship. There is no manipulation involved because there is nothing secretive, and your husband will also be able to choose his own behavior. This is not parenting. This is *partnering*. Your husband wants to have a close relationship with you, but has become a victim of his own behavior. He may not know emotionally how much his behavior has put him in danger of losing you.

You Have the Freedom to Give Up

You could choose to leave your husband, with some justification, because his behaviors are bad. That is your decision and I can't make it for you. I only point out that you are free to make it. Until you realize you have that freedom, you won't be able to see your helping him as a free choice. Since you don't have to be with him, you also don't have to help him. And when you do, it won't be because his behavior *makes* you. It will be because you love him enough to really try.

If you do decide to leave him as a method of motivating him (against my advice), he will probably choose at that moment to promise changes. His motivation to change will soar, but his ability to change will still be low, without your help and your persistence in the relationship. So, even if you separate, you still have to decide whether to help him or not. A man truly cannot fix a relationship all by himself, even if he is the one who has been causing the problems.

I won't take the divorce choice away from you, if it gives you comfort to hold it, because it doesn't have to be plan A or even plan B. It can be like a fighter pilot's ejector seat—something you hope never to use, but there just in case. In the meantime, you can choose to help your husband to change and to be able to be close to you. Good boundaries, not participating in the problem, making sure your husband's bad ways don't work with you, and knowing how to help him be successful with you, will be the methods you use to make your relationship truly wonderful.

If your husband has become a difficult man, and he used to be an "easy" man, then why isn't he changing back by himself? That he should change back is obvious. He was more likeable, and more loveable before he became so difficult. Perhaps he still has times when he is rather loveable now, but then he goes and spoils it with some kind of difficult behavior.

Why He Won't Change by Himself

As you read earlier, *changes* in character are not due to genetics. They could be due to biological changes such as illness, but are more often: 1) an adaptation (to home, work, family, etc.), and 2) a result of habit and identity as a such-and-such kind of person. "I am a man who ..." "can handle stress," " who should be king of the castle," "who doesn't show his feelings," etc. Those are the ways he is used to seeing himself. Those are the ways he is used to doing things. In other words, he does what has worked for him throughout his lifetime. Everything that he has done before has allowed him to come as far as he has. That's pretty good evidence to his mind, that his ways are the right way.

Although he is aware there are other ways to do things (which you may even have repeatedly pointed out to him), he has not had success with those ways (mainly because he has never given them a long enough trial). I don't know how many times I have heard a man say, "I tried talking to her. It didn't work." They are quick to condemn ways which are not theirs, without even stopping to realize that their way is not working either. Getting him to realize that will be necessary before he will change.

Your husband is also not applying the same skills as earlier in your relationship either because the situation has changed and he is dealing with it the best he can; or, because he *thinks* the situation has changed (e.g. "You're my wife, not my girlfriend, so I don't have to be nice"). Whenever you *tell* him to change, it is a source of frustration, anger, and sadness for him, because he believes he is already doing his best. Depending on the type of man he is, he will either turn his anger out at you, avoid the whole subject (and you), or shut down. The man who says, "You're probably right. Let's take a look at it and see what kind of changes I can make," is NOT a difficult man.

Choosing to Help is Not a One Time Choice

People continue to do what works for them, even if it only works a little (like driving a clunky car). This explains many human behaviors from gambling to alcoholism to spousal abuse. It explains why *you* continue to do many of the things you do, even though they maintain your problems, and even though you know what you *should* do. Although you are different from your husband in many ways, you are more alike than you are different. For example, you both have a great potential to change and to be any way that you want to be. And, for both of you, the unconscious pull to return to what you are used to doing (your habits) will threaten do derail you. New habits don't take hold until you have new success and maintain it. Anyone who achieves success is easily able to leave old ways behind.

The middle spot between survival and success is where 99% of people give up on their goals. Change doesn't bring instant success. You have to hang in there. When you understand that the desire to quit is part of the process of change and *a step closer to change*, it can encourage you to go on. "I feel like quitting, so I must be making progress." People who don't know this, experience the desire to quit as a sign of failure. Feeling like quitting is actually a natural by-product of change. There is no successful person who hasn't gone through some time when she felt like giving up. Whatever you are good at now, at one time you weren't. You had to push through the learning process before you got good at it and enjoyed it.

What usually stops people from quitting is *necessity*. Change becomes necessary when what they are doing is no longer working at all, so they *have to* change. Like when the clunky car dies, when they *have to* get a new job, when they *have to* be nice, or when they *have to* pay their bills. Using the methods in this book, you will make it so that your husband *has to* change. Because you are going to make sure that his ways break down. He's not going to be able to squeak by on behavior which is mostly bad. You are not going to settle for scraps of love and attention. Settling for scraps would allow him to be partially successful with bad behaviors and actually make it very difficult for him to change. You will learn to stop him and help him to have more success with you and to enjoy his relationship with you. Can you do that? Yes, you can.

Your husband puts on his pants one leg at a time because that's what works. If it didn't work, he would put them on a different way. And, whatever difficult behavior he is doing now, works for him, at least part of the time. It is important that you understand that. It works for him on either a psychological or a physical level. It maintains the world that he is used to (even if he doesn't like it). A negative person continues to be negative because that's the way he sees the world and that's the way he fits into what he sees. It is adaptation. Choosing to help your husband will entail learning why his behavior works with you at least part of the time, and changing the situation so that it *never* works with you. The answer to "Why does my husband..." is always "Because he can," and *not* "Because he wants to."

What *His* Choices Will Be

When what people do no longer works, they revert to doing what they used to do, even if it was long ago. All of our old habits are like built in back-up plans in case something is not working in our life. Many people are dismayed at their own behavior, when after years of being successful, they lose it, and do something they haven't done in years. Something wasn't working in their life, or they suddenly ran into something they haven't had to deal with for years. Then an old habit got triggered. It's only when people have no backup plan, or their old way will no longer work (like having a tantrum in the department store), that they seek out help. They feel desperate, lost, and confused. They are then ready to learn something new. Is it any wonder then, that people don't change much? Real change takes real ignorance, an understanding that you don't know what to do, or real failure, an understanding that your way is just not going to work. Success can follow either one of those paths because they open the mind up for learning.

What would happen if you tried to strong-arm your husband into changing? To just use brute emotional force such as threatening to divorce? He may be nice to you as he was in the past, because that worked before. Or, he may act out old family patterns that you haven't seen before. He learned somewhere, sometime, how to deal with feelings of rejection. Every behavior your husband has, he has learned. He doesn't make them up on the spot. And most of the things that he is doing now are *better* than the things he used to do. For example, faced with brute emotional force an ex-alcoholic may crawl back into the bottle. That, he knows how to do. Or, if he has really learned that alcohol doesn't work, then he may not return to the bottle. He may just get to the point where he does not know what to do (a good point if you can help him from there). But, it's very unpredictable. It's not worth the risk to use such strong-arm tactics unless you have nothing else and your relationship depends on it. Brute emotional force and strong-arm tactics are not ones you will learn in this book. A loving approach, with firm boundaries, should be sufficient.

If your husband's behavior is hard for you but the only other way he knows is to find a different woman, guess what he is going to do when his way no longer works with you? This doesn't mean that he has any desire to find another woman now. And if his old way of finding another woman didn't work either (e.g. trouble getting another woman), he could withdraw into depression, act out in violence, or avoid with addictions. These ways don't have to be learned. They are built in. They are primitive survival methods that don't require prior experience. They are the last resort efforts of our brains to help us survive. If you are attacked by a bear, you will react, prior experience or not. Many young men and women are quick to fall into anger and despair because of their lack of previous experience with loss. Can you remember that happening to you with your first romance?

The methods in this book, while they do require you to be firm, to hold your ground, and persist, are not strong-arm methods. Every time you give your husband a firm "no" to his behavior, you will also give him a "yes" to getting what he wants. There will be no need for him to fall back on old habits. The man who wants control gets to have control, but he does not get to be a bully. The man who is filled with jealousy, gets to be reassured, but not by interrogating you. The man who has made you a low priority gets to do his favorite things, but not by neglecting you. You will actually get more of what you want by helping him to have what he wants—while setting good boundaries. I will show you how to do that.

In this book, you will learn what motivates your husband and how to change your responses to him so that the way you get along changes. You will also learn how to help him to have more success and to be a better man without being a wimpy man. There is no need for him to keep his tail between his legs. You will help him at first without his cooperation, but then you will work more and more as a team. No one wants to cooperate in running into a wall. And that's what will happen when he uses his bad behaviors with you. But, when he starts getting more and more of what he wants (love and a good relationship with you), you will wonder why you didn't do this a long time ago.

The reason that books and marriage retreats and even counseling usually fail to change difficult men's behavior is their bad behaviors continue to work. And because their old habits still work, too. If your husband tries to drill a hole into cement with a drill bit designed for wood, will he stop and go get the correct bit? Well, it depends on whether he is making progress. If the wood bit is working, then he probably won't change it. If it just turns without making a hole, he will soon stop using it. Your husband's mind is geared to keep going until he hits a brick wall and then to go through it, if possible.

With easy men, you can give them the right tool, show them how to use it and problem solved. With difficult men, hand them the right tool and they will be reluctant to use it. They will if they have to. But only after they try six other ways that don't work. And, they are not likely to say, "Gosh Hon, you were right all along. Whew, I should have listened to you and saved myself all the trouble." You can save that kind of expectation for your fantasies. Difficult men do things, but they do them the hard way. Especially if the hard way has worked for them before. One realistic way to look at your husband's difficult behavior is to look at him as having a relationship with you *the hard way*.

Compromise, or Give-in?

As you help your husband to have more and more success the easy way and as he begins to receive what he wants (an important piece of the puzzle), he will become more and more interested in working with you. Men can become downright *excited* when they realize that they can have more and more of what they want as women help them to get more and more of what they want. What they want always includes a good relationship with you, among other things, so it's not a big risk even if some of the things they want seem really goofy. This is an application of the win-win principle. I win when you win. So I want you to win. That cannot be achieved with compromise.

With compromise, you lose something and I lose something. Win-win adds energy. Compromise takes it away. Think about whether you have been compromising with your husband and whether that has been adding to or taking away from your relationship. When you compromise with him, does he become more eager to work with you? Or does he seem more like a dog who accepts a biscuit when he was hoping for a pork chop? Many people are surprised to find that compromise is for keeping peace—it's not for getting close. There is no excitement in compromise.

Make Things Fair or Make Things Good?

I hope you're not still saying at this point that it's "not fair" if you have to help your husband, because he is treating you badly. Fairness is for the courtroom and it never makes anyone happy. Fairness is making sure nobody gets what they deserve. Or that everyone gets what they deserve. Either way, it is trouble. Love has little to do with fairness. *Love* is the characteristic that is most needed when someone is hurting you. By helping your husband to have success with a new and better way, you will be loving not only him, but yourself. This is because helping him to change creates a better relationship for the both of you. It certainly isn't possible to create a better relationship just for yourself!

Loving "for better or for worse" doesn't mean that we love it when things are worse, but that we continue to love even when things are worse. The way we show love for anyone is to do what is in his best interest. In your husband's case, it is helping him to have a better relationship with you. (If you don't think that's in his best interest, then either you need to work on your self-esteem or your behavior toward him).

The following chapters will teach you about the motivations different types of difficult men have. They will also teach you how to make your husband's difficult behaviors fail with you, while also helping him to get what he really wants. You will learn to lead, at least temporarily. This is because you can't follow his lead and make progress (as you can see in your relationship). Also, he cannot lead you to a better place when he doesn't know how to go there himself.

Your biggest enemy to change won't be your husband. He will welcome it once things get rolling. Your biggest enemy to change will be *your* desire to return to your old ways before you start having success with these new ways. That temptation happens in the in-between learning time, when you are emotionally sore, and before you see improvement. All I can say to you is that while many people do give up, some people don't. Some people succeed the first time around, but most don't. Some people are able to make the changes on their own without support, and some people need extra help. But all of these people can succeed—except for the ones who give up.

These are not reasons to be frightened off. They are reasons to make you aware that if things don't go well the first time, then they will the second or third and that they can go even easier with the right help and support. I hope you put counseling or coaching as a higher level backup plan than the plan for divorce (if you are holding that in reserve). Now, you should be ready to go ahead. You're working plan should be to make the changes in this book while getting support from your friends. Your backup plan is to get professional help and support. Your ejector seat plan is to divorce or breakup (if it makes you feel better to have it). The thing that we most definitely will not plan is for you to continue to endure your relationship, unchanged, until doomsday.

"I am extraordinarily patient, provided I get my own way in the end." Margaret Thatcher

4

WHY DO MEN MESS UP RELATIONSHIPS?

Asking "Why?" can hurt or help, depending on who you ask. "Why" is one of the most perplexing of all questions. After our partner answers a "why" question, we are usually no more certain about the reason than before. The most common question in counseling is *"How* do you feel about that?" rather than *"Why* do you do that?" This isn't because the counselor or coach doesn't care why, but because "why" stimulates defensiveness while blocking solutions. "Why did you yell at her?" "Because I was mad" "Why were you mad?" "Because she was being selfish," "Why do you think she was being selfish?" "Because she's always selfish." Circular reasoning—a dead end. Ask his wife the why question, and you get the same type of answers. After which they feel even less like working with each other. "Why's" get defensive reactions because people feel interrogated, put on the spot, like they are being accused. Defensiveness disconnects people. Usually when couples use the "why" word with each other, it has the same effect. There are, however, some good ways to use "why."

It's good to ask *ourselves* "why" about our *partner's* feelings. Such as, "Why is he angry?" "Why is he worried?" Or "Why is he sad?" The "why" question can help you to think about your partner's perspective, taking your focus off your partner's behavior, putting it on his feelings, allowing you to have greater empathy with him. We can't sympathize with controlling behavior, but we can sympathize with the fear behind the controlling behavior. We can't sympathize

47

with withdrawal, but we can sympathize with the desire to protect oneself that causes him to withdraw.

We can also use the "why" question to understand our partner's perspective about us, though we have to be careful not to be defensive when we hear it. For example, if you ask, "Why do you think I yell at you when you come home late?" He may answer, "Because you don't care about my life, just your own." Although his answer may be inaccurate, it right away identifies the basis of his insecurity—"You don't *care* about me," a fear that you don't care about him, expressed in an attacking way. If you can listen to the fear and ignore the attack, it is an opportunity to deepen your relationship by: 1) helping him to feel cared about, and 2) to remind you to work on having good limits rather than yelling when he returns late. Reducing his fears while using good boundaries will bring the closeness and behavior change you want to see in him.

When you understand more of the "whys" of your husband's behavior, you will see him more as he really is, and not as a crazy, chaotic person, who behaves badly for no good reason. Understanding can help you to not see him as the enemy. He has reasons for his behavior that, if better understood, can help you to sympathize with him, even if they don't give you an immediate solution. That sympathy can help you keep a loving perspective as you work on changing his difficult and unacceptable behaviors. It can help you to focus on helping rather than reacting.

I will go through some general "why's" with you now to help you understand your husband's behavior. In each of the following chapters I will also explore some more specific reasons for men's behavior. They may help you to understand his behavior better than he understands it himself.

Biology Isn't the Answer

Some things are characteristic of all men due to their common biology. Without a common biology, they couldn't be classified as men at all. We have moved past the era of believing that men and women are basically the same. They aren't, as you well know from your experience with them. We have also moved past the era of saying that women are inferior to men. They aren't. But, we now must make one more stride and get past the idea that men are emotionally inferior to women. They aren't. Men and women are simply different. When they combine their differences, as in a good marriage, the result can be superior to what a single man or woman can do alone.

Although all men share a common biology, they differ widely in the way they express their emotions. These differences are what create difficult men.

Let's consider anger as one example. Although when men are angry, adrenaline fuels their engines, it doesn't steer their behavior. It makes them feel like doing something, but they still decide what to do based on their history, culture, and experience. For that reason, men in Western cultures are much more likely to punch a wall than their wife, or their TV. Most will rarely or never punch anything at all, even if they feel that way. Angry men are not biologically different from their more patient peers. Men who hit, shout, and control can't blame their testosterone or adrenaline levels. They express their emotions differently because there's something different about their thinking process.

Along the same line of reasoning, biological differences are **not** responsible for your husband treating you unfairly, being insecure, or having a lack of concern for you. He is biologically powered the same as all men (overpowered or underpowered, at times), and it is his judgment which decides how that power is used. If he makes poor decisions, he needs help making better ones. Unless he can't function, he does not need to be adjusted by medication, whether prescription or not.

You also won't need to control or overpower his urges; you do need to direct and guide him. It may help you to imagine you are like the painted lines on a highway, directing and guiding, making things safer, but allowing your husband to maintain complete control over his own behavior. It's his choice to stay within the lines or not, but cross over them and his relationship is at risk, likely to be damaged. The "guide lines" (boundaries) you put in place will need to be designed according to his particular behaviors.

Insecure Self Image

Some men behave the way they do because they are not quite sure if they really measure up to the way they believe they are supposed to be. For instance, they may be trying to "act like a man." Men who are comfortable with themselves (for better or worse), don't try to act like anything—including other people's stereotypes of how they are supposed to be. But, many men are insecure in their masculinity.

49

These men are careful not to do things which could make anyone think they are not "masculine" (whatever that is). This behavior becomes most notable in public places and especially around other men. Many macho types of men are influenced in this way.

There are two basic ways to deal with men who have this kind of problem. One is to draw the line between what you will and will not tolerate. In public, don't try to stop him from being whatever he believes he needs to be. He can be the clown, the boor, the bully, to his heart's content, but not with you. Because you will simply refuse to participate when he behaves that way. You will take control of your behavior (not his) and leave the *instant* he becomes that way. He is free to beat up on the waiter at the restaurant, but he will be dining alone while you take a taxi home. Your behaving this way means the end of codependence. Done early enough in a relationship, it nips such behavior in the bud. Done later on, consistently, it prunes out unacceptable behavior.

When you prune, you must also water. This is the second way of dealing with this type of problem in men. You do this by helping him to feel more secure in his masculinity. The more secure he feels, the less he will need to "act" like a man. When you talk about men, make sure to say the characteristics you want him to have. Don't say, "men are so rude," unless you want him to become more rude. Remember, good or bad, he is trying to live up to your image of what a man is as well. It's better to say something like, "men really know what they want," or "men have a good ability to focus and get the job done," etc. While women have wider freedom in whether they express their femininity or not, most women want to "feel like a woman" at least some of the time. And their male partners can help them to feel that way by what they say and do. What you say and do with your partner can also help him to feel manly. Most men, and especially difficult ones, want to feel like men *most* of the time.

Self-Image is Much More than Being a Man

Self-image is important to all of us. We need a stable sense of self to make sense of the world and to guide our behavior. So we behave in ways which preserve the way we see ourselves. And, we get other people to respond to us in a way that helps us preserve our self-image. Other people are the social mirror for our self-image.

A man who believes he is no good at talking to women, won't talk to women very often. And he will continue to have communication problems with women. This in turn will get him poor responses from women, which will confirm his beliefs about himself. On the other hand, convince him that he really is good at talking to women, and he really will become better at it. Then he will get better responses from others, which will show him he can talk to women. What we believe influences what we do and helps to maintain our habits. That's why helping your husband to believe he is a loving husband is so important. Cursing creates curses; loving creates lovers. Your words do shape him, just as his words shape you.

When people do things that are not consistent with the way they see themselves, it creates an internal tension that must be explained.[1] If a law abiding citizen, throws a rock through a store window, he will need to have some way to explain that to himself. He will look for and grab onto any reason which helps him preserve his belief that he is a law abiding citizen. He is likely to be open to the idea that the stress of life got to him and he cracked, if only for a moment. It wasn't like him—it was an exception. A man who mistreats his wife, but sees himself as a good husband, must either blame his wife, his situation, or both. That is much more tolerable to him than to change his beliefs about himself. Self-image, and our desire to have a good one, are the main reasons we defend so strongly, even when we are wrong. Even when we *know* we are wrong.

If your husband does not see himself as a good husband, helping him to see himself as one will make it easier for him to change bad behavior, and harder for him to stay a difficult man. When we criticize people, it helps them to maintain negative beliefs about themselves. Then they continue to behave in ways consistent with those beliefs. We can create bad children by telling them that they are bad. Tell a man enough times that he is a slob and you are more likely to get an even bigger slob as a result. This is because after a while, he will believe you. Help him to see himself as an organized man (for example, in his work, tool collection, or the way he arranges his music collection) and he becomes more and more likely to pick up his socks as well. Some people think of this as a woman "taming" a man, but I think of it as a woman helping her man to be the best he can be. And, he will love you for it. How would you feel about a man who believes in you, encourages you, and sees in you something

---

[1] Festinger, L. (1957). *A theory of cognitive dissonance*. Stanford, CA: Stanford University Press.

better than you see in yourself? Wouldn't such a man bring out the best in you? Is that taming? Or training? Isn't it part of loving and being a good partner?

The interesting thing about self-image is that we have it about everything (e.g. "this is the way I butter my toast"), except for new experiences. The way we dress, eat, talk to people, walk, think about things, feel about things, etc. is programmed into our identity. Most of our behaviors and even the things we think about are a result of habit, habit being our underlying identity. We can describe what people are like because of their consistency in thought, behavior, and appearance. And people can describe you, too. People know what you are like. This consistency allows us to run on autopilot most of the time. The things your husband usually does, happen with very little thought on his part. He doesn't plot against you, he just acts out of habit, with very little thought at all. To change him, he first has to be made aware of his own bad behavior.

Because habits don't work in unfamiliar situations, when we are in an *unfamiliar* situation, we suddenly think about what to do or say and how others are reacting to us. We quickly gather clues from others that let us know whether our behavior is acceptable or not. When we are in Rome, we look to see what the Romans are doing. That is why your husband probably behaves very differently at work and at home. He has learned that what works socially in one place is not what works in the other. He then has a different self-image for each of those places. He has an image of what it is to be a good worker and an image of what it is to be a good husband. He may talk to the office ladies more nicely than he ever talks to you. The more different his work image and his home image are, the less he will want to mix the two. You showing up at his workplace could be a very stressful surprise. By the same token, his coworkers or colleagues might be shocked at the way he behaves at home.

The principle of adaptation in unfamiliar territory is something you can use to help him change. When you change the routine interactions that you have with each other, you are putting him into unfamiliar territory, switching off his autopilot, forcing him to create new behavior.

A young man, with few relationship habits, is easier to change than a middle aged man. His self-image, his "autopilot" hasn't been fully developed yet. People get "set" in their ways only after they operate in the same environment for a long time. Then, they demand you conform to their "set" rather than adapt to you. It can be a battle of autopilots, complete with habitual "auto fighting." Fortunately, even with such a "set," pre-programmed man, there are many ways for you to create change, starting with making sure his autopilot breaks down. To put it another way, when there are no old habits, new habits can easily form. When there are old habits, they have to stop working before new ones can form. This includes the way he treats you. Fortunately, you have a lot of control over how well his habits work with you. It is your behavior that allows him to stay on autopilot or not.

Changing Habits

Working to change habits is harder than learning something new. That is true of ourselves, as well as our partners. If I wanted to change my daily routine, it would be much easier for me to do that in a new context. If I moved far away or changed jobs, putting myself into unfamiliar territory, I would have new friends who influence what I do and how I think about things. If I made several changes, like moving to a new country, getting a new job, and making new friends, I might change so much that I would seem to have a different personality. And this is precisely what happens to many people who move overseas. When they are visited by their friends from their home country, their friends notice big changes. They have created a new self-image that fits their new location. If you have an international marriage and you return with your husband to his home country, expect to see some behavior, or even personality, changes. He will fall back on old habits in old situations (like with family).

I'm going to teach you how to help your husband develop better habits, mainly by creating new situations. You will do this merely by changing the way you respond to him. In a way, it will be like he is getting a new, healthier woman, with better boundaries, but who loves him dearly. Because he only knows how to deal with the current you, he will *have to* adjust. Every change you make in yourself, or your way of doing things will require a change (an adaptation) on his part. This is not a new process in your relationship. You, after all, have adjusted to his changes little by little, until you have become the way you are now. Your husband didn't ask you to do that. You had no choice but to change. The difference this time, is that he will be adjusting to you. Because the changes you will be making are healthy ones, they will improve the relationship rather than make it worse.

Unfortunately, when you make changes, he will still have to go through the "growing pains" that come with adaptation. And you need to be ready for that. The first reaction he will have to any change you make is to do what he always does but even more intensely. His behavior will become *worse* as his autopilot goes to full power. After a while, his autopilot will run out of energy and fail altogether. Because you are aware of his habits, you can predict and prepare for this even worse behavior. We don't need to be upset when we can predict and prepare.

Knowing something about what motivates him will help you to make changing easier for him, decreasing the time it takes for him to adjust. Just as it is less difficult to accept a new job if it has more benefits—more of what we want—changing and adaptation can also be rewarding for him.

The Four Primary Motivators of Difficult Men

Drs. Brinkman and Kirschner[2] have identified four psychological needs that strongly influence how we interact with other people. These four needs are: 1) the need to get things done, 2) the need to get things right, 3) the need to get appreciation, and, 4) the need to get along. The researchers say that we each have all four of these needs. We function best when these needs are in balance. When we are emotionally healthy we don't try overly hard to get appreciation or to get everything right. We do try to get along, but not so much that we don't get anything done.

However, the researchers go on to say that when we are under stress, one of these four needs becomes stronger according to our personality. We become more needy in a particular motivation and get more upset when that need is not met. Under stress, some people will have a greater need for appreciation while others will focus more on making sure things are just right; still others will become more concerned about getting along, or become more concerned about getting things done. Accordingly, some men will get very angry with you if they see you as standing in the way of their getting something done. Others will stop trying to get things done,

---

[2] Brinkman, R. and Kirschner, R. (2003). *Dealing with difficult people: 24 Lessons for bringing out the best in anyone.* New York: McGraw-Hill.

and even let them go undone, as they get more obsessed with getting appreciation or getting along. Some small "sign" from you that the relationship is not just right can trigger a number of angry or depressed responses. Perhaps you were just tired when you didn't smile at his joke, but his need to get along was so great that he overreacted.

The implication is, you need to know which need your husband is trying to meet when he is stressed, and take that into account in your communication. Working with your husband on *getting along*, when he is focused on *getting things done*, will just create more conflict. If you show him how to get things done by working on getting along, it will appeal more to what he desires (although it amounts to the same thing). That is, you can get more of what you want (a good relationship) by appealing to his needs and stating things in terms of his desires. For example, what kind of man is going to respond well to this question, "How can I help you?" Answer—the man with a strong need to get things done. Who is going to respond best to, "I really admire the way you care what happens to me"? Answer—the man with the need for appreciation. Say the same thing to men with different needs and you may get a blank reaction or even a hostile one. It will be as if you two are not on the same wavelength. And you will each feel as though the other just doesn't "get it."

If you say things to help your husband without getting any good results, consider that you may not have identified his strongest needs correctly. Such concepts will be used heavily in this book since each type of man tends to have different types of social needs. It is an area where we need to pay special attention because his social needs connect him to you. This is also a reminder that you and your husband may both desire a closer relationship but for different reasons. One of you may delight in getting things done while the other delights in getting along. There is no reason you can't have both. Cooperating, you can.

The need to "get things right," when taken to an extreme is perfectionism. In certain occupations, perfectionism is mandatory, such as in surgery, bookkeeping, and engineering. Close enough just isn't good enough. If you are married to a man who works in a field demanding precision, he may well have a need to get things right. This tendency will be responsible for some of his occupational success, although it may also cause relational problems. His eye for detail may mean that he comes off as critical, and you may get the feeling that no matter how hard you try, what you do is never good enough.

A man with a strong need to get things right can take a very long time to take any kind of action as he must gather a lot of information and weigh all possibilities before taking any actions—lest he make some kind of error. This means that although he may recognize the need for things to change, he is unlikely to change quickly, and to want proof of success before he tries something new. What you see as stubborn, he may see as careful. What you see as worth trying, he may see as reckless. And, because stress accentuates needs, the more stressed he is, the harder it is for him to come to decisions and the more critical he will be. The reverse is also true, making him more easy going and less careful when he is relaxed, such as when he drinks. Here lies one of the dangers.

The need to "get things done" is characteristic of a man of action. He may well be a leader, ready to take risks and action before all information is collected. He will gravitate toward people who help him get things done and run over people who stand in his way. If he is trying to get somewhere or do something, and you stand in his way, watch out! Under stress, something as small as a slow checkout line at the store could get him upset. If your husband is like this, it probably helps him to be successful in many ways. It probably doesn't help your communication though, when you are trying to explain something to him and he just wants the bottom line. You can learn how to put his need to get things done to good use for both of you, while also learning to deal with his aggressive behaviors. You might even be able to help him see how he can get more done by listening to you.

A man with a strong "need to get along" may sound ideal for relationships. Unfortunately, when this need is not balanced with the others, too often too little gets done or things are done in a careless way and very many practical problems result. He may also make conflicting promises to different people. Putting stress on this kind of man to get things done or to do things better will probably result in his agreement, but not in his taking action. He is much more likely than the previous two kinds of men (need to get things done, and need to get things right) to be passive and avoidant. He may often tell you "yes, you are right" and then not follow through. Rather than behaving like a demanding father, he is more likely to behave like an immature son. Many of these men, in fact, still have a very strong parent-child relationship with their biological parents. The need to get along is important for them to be able to survive with other very difficult people who call the shots in their life. It may also serve them well in their jobs, even if they secretly hate their bosses (or clients). "Yes Men," and "Mama's Boys," both tend to have agreeable attitudes and thinly hidden resentment. If your husband is like this, his desire to get along with you is genuine and will be helpful as you work on improving your relationship with him. But, you will need to learn how to light the fire under him without burning yourself on his resentment.

The "need to get appreciation" is also something we all have. Who can feel like he or she really matters without appreciation? When we get positive attention for doing things that other people enjoy, it is a win-win. We can notably think of politicians, actors, and football players, for example. These people are interesting and talented and other people enjoy giving them attention. Your husband, regardless of his other needs, also has a need for appreciation and has learned to get positive attention and appreciation in at least some key areas. If he is one of the men who is *primarily* motivated by the need for appreciation, and he feels most appreciated outside the home (work, by others, etc.), then he will even more energetically pursue things other than your relationship with him.

The solution for this kind of man is not simply to give him appreciation. It is to help him to get positive attention and appreciation for pro-social behavior, especially in his relations with you. You can't increase positive behavior simply by ignoring bad behavior. You must make a way for him to get positive attention and appreciation as you take away attention, and set good boundaries for, negative things. When men say that "women are too much work," they are often talking about how much they have to do to get a little appreciation. Men who desire appreciation, and feel appreciated, are usually willing to do a lot without complaint.

The Worse the Problem, the Faster the Change

Regardless of personality types, self-image, or characteristic needs, you will not see positive change immediately, no matter what your intervention. This is because when his autopilot becomes useless, it will take time for him to realize that. How do you know something will not work one time in 25 unless you try 25 times? Remember, people continue to do whatever brings them partial success, even if that is not very often. And when you stop your husband from having success (for example in pushing your buttons), he won't realize your buttons no longer work until he pushes them many more times. If the mouse for your computer stopped working, how many times would you click it to make sure it's not working? My guess is you would click it many times as well as unplugging it and plugging it back in. Then you would try restarting your computer multiple times. Finally, you would realize that your mouse really no longer works. If it worked a little the next day, you might again try it many times. That mouse button is like your own "buttons." He's not going to stop pushing them until he's sure they no longer work.

The *less* often his bad behavior occurs, the *longer* it will take to change. If your husband is used to getting his way (effectively pushing your button) only once a week, then he may need 8 to 12 weeks to catch on that it is just not working anymore. On the other hand, if your husband is used to getting his way every day, he will learn within 1 to 2 weeks that it doesn't work anymore, once you start using good boundaries. This has the interesting result that frequent and severe problems can be changed much faster than infrequent and mild problems. If you have a really difficult husband, this is good news!

Even with mild problems, though, change can occur within three months. To do this, whenever you are changing the way you respond to your husband, you will need to be consistent in your response, and not assume your intervention is not working, until three months have passed. By far, stopping too soon is where most people fail and where you can succeed. To stick with it, you will need to have your own effective coping responses or your own needs (for appreciation, to get it done, to get it right, or to get along), will drive you to revert to your old habits. If you do that, all the old, bad patterns will start again between you and your husband. The coming chapters will therefore help you with your needs while you help your husband with his. In this way you can both be more successful and get more of what you both really want—a better relationship.

5

HE CHANGED—SO WHY SHOULD I STAY WITH HIM?

Every day I work with women who want to have a better relationship with a difficult man. But, I have never met a woman who said she wanted to *start* a relationship with a difficult man. And, if your husband has changed, is no longer loving, cherishing, or honoring you, why should you stay with him? In this chapter, I will not only answer this question, I will also help you to understand why things have gone wrong so long in your relationship without changing. At least, not changing for the better.

He Wasn't Always This Way

Clearly men don't announce they are difficult when you first date them, and if they have any awareness of their problems, they do their best to hide them. While some men are "players," with a hidden agenda, they are not the topic of this book. Here we are considering the men who have lovingly committed themselves to a relationship with a woman. Typically, they do not have a hidden agenda. They are honestly wanting to commit to the women they commit to because they love them and want to spend their life with them. It is no surprise, then, that many women fall in love with them. Usually women with difficult husbands did not overlook a glaring flaw when they married their husbands.

Some women do get married too quickly and some marry even in the face of glaring problems—hoping things will get better. If you are such a woman, we *can* say "You made a mistake." Even so, intervention methods like the ones in this book can still work for you. Women who made such early mistakes need to recognize that it was not all his fault. Although you may have missed some warning signs, his emotions and desire to commit to you were real. He respected the boundaries that you set, or else you would not have continued with him. If your boundaries were poor, he is not to blame for that. Even if you had very good boundaries, you may not have had the chance to see any warning signs. The conflicts and issues you have with him now may not have been there at that time. Finding another man now, no matter how careful you are, could put you right back in the same place. The place to look for the answer is *not* at the beginning—with your selection process. The place to look is at the time he changed.

Special Alert about Men Who Changed Quickly

A small minority of women have wonderful relationships with their husbands until one day, poof!, their husband has a sudden major personality change. They have no reason to explain it, and they didn't see it coming. In these cases, I would recommend counseling by a psychologist or psychiatrist rather than starting with the methods in this book. A medical reason for the drastic change needs to be ruled out. It does happen, and when it does, it is usually very serious. Don't mess around in such a sudden change situation. Strokes, chemical poisoning, and head injuries to name a few can cause such change. One of the men I saw for couples counseling had such a change due to heavy metals in his blood from his work place exposure. Drastic changes often have drastic reasons and are not particularly characteristic of difficult men.

Gradual Change Can Also Result from Physical and Emotional Disorders

Along the same lines, the gradual onset of serious psychological and medical disorders can also bring about a change in personality and behavior. The brain is an organ of our body and it is also what we use to think and interact. Biological conditions impact the health of the brain, which impacts thoughts and decisions. Just consider the last time you had a bad cold. How energetic did you feel? How happy were you? How much did you feel like doing things with your husband? What happened to your sex drive? The number one reason men lose interest in having sex is fatigue. Fatigue lands a heavy blow on other feelings as well. If his mood or energy level are very different on his days off from work for example, it could indicate a sleeping problem.

Gradual Change with No Medical Cause

If you are among the majority of women with difficult husbands, your husband was a very fine catch, or so you thought at the time. Things gradually got worse over a period of years. There is also good evidence that it is not a health problem or psychological disorder, because he enjoys himself with other people and has plenty of energy to do the things he wants to do. It's hard for you to put a finger on just when things started to go wrong, though you might remember a few major incidents.

Sometimes the downhill slide starts with an event, but is not recognized as such at the time. It can be your getting a job, his changing jobs, the birth of a child, buying a house, moving, loss of a friend, or any other environmental change. Like a pebble tossed in a pond, these causes can send ripples out, which cause bigger and bigger problems as time goes by. Husband gets a new job... makes more money... works longer hours... gets more tired... gets more interested in vegetating in front of the TV than talking to his wife. Wife tries to be patient and understanding... gradually gets emotionally emptied... becomes increasingly irritable with her husband. Husband reacts in a *previously uncharacteristic way* to preserve his space and de-stress (explodes, withdraws, or acts out). Wife, shocked, angered, and turned off by his behavior, reacts defensively. Obviously, this is only one of a hundred possible scenarios. The point is to see how small changes can set off a chain of events and reactions. Even if the husband in this scenario went back to his old job, the ripples would continue to cause problems. The damage would still be there. We can't undo problems by returning to past behaviors. Who was at fault? Both of them? Neither of them? Who can say? The important thing is becoming close again. Then all those conflicts that are rippling out won't really matter that much and will fade away. This is the main goal of relationship coaching—to build closeness first, dealing only with major obstacles, rather than working on all the little ripples (the problems). Any problems that remain will be much easier to deal with when you and your husband feel close and are talking cooperatively.

Stopping the Downward Slide

Most couples will make attempts to improve their relationship when it becomes bad for both of them. But as long as one person is satisfied, very little usually happens except for the unhappy partner becoming even more unhappy. An unhappy partner can provoke a satisfied partner to unhappiness, of course. And that is usually what happens. A person who feels like she is getting little will usually give little in return. Eventually both husband and wife will feel depleted and resentful. With teamwork or counseling, the couple may renew their relationship.

Difficult men, though, are not known for their teamwork or cooperation with counseling. Even when they attend counseling, they often find a way to sabotage it. Or, worse yet, the counselor finds it easier to empathize with the wife and the difficult husband feels ganged up on. Keep in mind that regardless of how bad your husband's behavior is, a good counselor or coach will not take sides.

Women often receive *support* in counseling if they attend without their husband, but may not find *solutions* other than to leave their husband. Your husband's fear of your attending counseling may be quite valid. He may sense that your counselor would *not* discourage you from leaving him. Counselors often feel they can't help someone they don't see. The exception is family systems counselors. Although they often work with as many people in a family who will participate, they also work without the presence of the "identified patient" (the person in the family who has the most problems). They know that the behaviors of that person are in part maintained by the behaviors of the other family members (Aylmer, 1986[3]; Todd, 1986[4]).

---

[3] Aylmer, R C. (1986). Bowen family systems marital therapy. In N. S. Jacobson & A. E. Gurman (Eds.), *Clinical handbook of marital therapy,* New York: Guilford,107-148.

[4] Todd, T. C. (1986). Structural-strategic marital therapy. In N. S. Jacobson & AS. Gurman (Eds.), *Clinical handbook of marital therapy,* New York: Guilford, 71-105.

You are part of a system, playing a part in patterns and cycles of behavior, with your husband (as well as others). When you change what you do, it changes those patterns. Just as when your husband changes what he does, it influences how you feel about, and respond to him.

Giving Up Is the Natural Next Step, but Not a Necessary One

For those who have separated or are in the process of a divorce, I think it's fair to say that they are choosing to no longer have a relationship with their difficult husband. Given a choice between living with a difficult husband or divorce it's hard to blame them. But there are other choices. A complicating factor is that later on, many of these women will reestablish their relationship with the same man (when he "promises" to be good) or another man who repeats the same pattern. The more times a woman experiences this real-life "re-run," the more she will be convinced that men are no good, that relationships are more work than they are worth, and that life is more like surviving the ride than enjoying it. How sad.

Some women come to the conclusion that something is wrong with them, which causes them to play the same role with different men. These women are partly right. They are not responsible for the men's behaviors, but they do keep failing to deal with men's behavior correctly. Learning to end such behavior will also end such patterns. They are not failures at love or relationships. They are just one step from having a really good one.

No Woman Is Doomed to Have Bad Relationships

There is no fundamental flaw in women that dooms them to have difficult relationships. Every woman can learn to have clear boundaries and healthy expectations for men. They can learn to recognize when they are being disrespected and stop such behavior. They can learn these things before they are in a committed relationship, and so make it easier on themselves by committing to a healthier man. Then their relationship won't slide far before they take action. Women can also learn to recognize and deal with such behaviors in an established relationship. There is actually a lot of satisfaction in doing so, and once learned, won't be forgotten. That's why changes made in coaching are permanent. Once we learn something well, we don't go back to our old ways. Once a person learns to ride a bike, she will never put her training wheels back on.

The Great Myth That All Men Are the Same

I have one question for women who believe that all men are the same. How can you explain that many women have good relationships with men if they are all the same? If all men are the same, and men are bad, then there must be something wrong with the women who love them and have good relationships with them! A much simpler explanation is that men and women are neither good nor bad. *Relationships* are either good or bad, depending on the way that the couple are relating to each other. Changing the way we relate, changes the relationship. Fortunately for us, normal, everyday, messed up people can have good relationships. You and your husband can relate well again without having to perfect each other.

The things that we do each day determine what happens the following day. If we continue to get the same results in life, it's because we continue to make the same choices and do the same things. Likewise, if our relationships with our spouses continue to be the same, it's because we continue to interact (initiate and respond) in the same way. The things that we need to do to change our relationships are completely under our control. You can make changes to yourself that he will react to. If you don't make any changes, but expect him to, nothing may ever change. Changing the way you interact with him will automatically change the way he interacts with you. This does not mean being patient, or enduring your situation, because that won't bring change. Being patient is not an action.

Trapped in a Bad Relationship

It may seem impossible to believe that some women would choose to continue a bad relationship, but it's only because they fall into invisible traps. Learning to see the trap is the first step toward getting out of it. Use the following information to identify which one you are in.

The Habit Trap

Probably the number one reason why women put up with bad behavior from their husbands is the same reason that their husbands have the bad behavior. It is their normal expectation, their belief, their idea of how to be a couple. They have seen many relationships with the same problems. On a subconscious level, it seems normal. Like a dog who is used to being chained in the backyard. The longer they have been this way, the more normal it will seem. People can consciously hate their relationship, yet out of habit continue the very behaviors that keep it bad. Good and bad habits are what get us through our days, hours, weeks, months, and years.

When we already have a developed habit, we will use it, even if we see other people behaving better. No one can change their habits by watching romantic movies. Habits are kind of automated programs that prevent us from having to continually figure out how to do things—how to think—and how to feel. That means that we will not be influenced to behave like people in TV shows or movies and so our relationships will not become like them. Nor do the fantasies about the relationship we would like to have express themselves in our actions. Thus, the lonely woman with poor social skills who dreams of being swept off her feet by a prince actually does nothing in her real life that would attract the most common of men, let alone a prince. She follows her habits. She remains invisible to all except men who are attracted to needy women.

So it is for the woman with a bad relationship. She doesn't like the way the relationship is, but she's gotten used to it—she has a habitual way of dealing (or not dealing) with it. In all likelihood, her relationship is not so different from that of her friends or family members. This is even more likely to be the case when she has married someone from within her home town, workplace, or school. No striking differences from her past and no striking differences from her peers means that she is very unlikely to stop and say, "Something is really wrong—my marriage is not supposed to be like this." Rather than question the way she and her husband relate, she is more likely just to conclude that she is an unhappy person or that "life sucks." Her "solution," if she thinks of one at all, may be to get another relationship. But, since she has never had a better relationship, she also won't have much motivation for divorcing and finding someone new. The "hassle" of changing outweighs the hurt of keeping things as they are. It is stuck-ness. And it feels like hopelessness. It's likely that her husband would think and feel pretty much the same (i.e., "life sucks, but what can you do?").

This same woman, were she to fall in love with and marry a very different man such as a foreigner, would be confronted with more than a thousand differences ranging from the way to fold socks to what religion is best for their family. Such a level of difference would be out of her norm. Changing relationships would then be for her less of a hassle than keeping a bad one and so her likely solution would be to divorce.

There are very few such differences for most women, whose husbands have grown up in very similar environments. Women are also more likely to mate with men who are similar in their beliefs than with those who are very different. This kind of relationship is well balanced, and stable. They will fight a lot if that is their habit or belief about how couples relate and resolve their differences. They will be passive, and avoidant, if that is their belief. When husband and wife match in their expectations this way and when the relationship is not good, it will nevertheless be stable. It can last for years or a lifetime. It will not occur to either of them that their relationship can actually be any different than it is. Romantic movies will just be fiction and close couples will just seem strange. Any thoughts of changing their relationship are likely to revolve around changing partners. "My life would be so much better if I only had someone else."

Rarely, though, does changing partners do anything to improve relationships, since people are drawn to, and match, the same kind of person they were with before. The more experience a man or woman has with relationships, the better he or she will become at attracting and selecting *exactly* the same kind of partner as before. All men are the same when you keep attracting the same kind. Women who have only dated aggressive men will think all men are aggressive. They are likely to also *not* be attracted to men who are gentle. They are not good at relationships with such men.

Women in negative, stable relationships, need to be very unhappy with their relationship to be willing to do something about it. At the same time, they need to have another model for improving relationships than divorce and remarriage. Most of the time husbands are also unhappy, but do not want divorce. They can be motivated to make changes if their wives can demonstrate to them how, and if they stop playing by the rules (the "rules" being their beliefs about how couples should relate). Husbands don't know how to relate better just because their wives demand it.

Because men respond to action rather than words, their wife's changes in behavior motivate more than talking ever will. Her new actions create a chance for both her and her husband to be happier. It gets them both unstuck. These are the kinds of actions that you will learn in this book. They are the actions you must take if you want your husband to change, and for the relationship to improve. Once men are motivated to change, they can be powerful allies for continued change, and the relationship can take on a new life. This is an excellent time for outside help because both husband and wife will be ready to work on positive changes, but can become discouraged if they don't make the right ones.

"Pleasing the Family" Trap

For several reasons, friends and family are not likely to support the kind of changes necessary to improve your relationship. In fact, they are even likely to oppose it—especially in the beginning. It will be at that time that some extra tension will be created (a necessary and healthy part of change), and to friends and family members, it will appear like things are getting worse. Don't bother to try to explain it to them—it won't help. Once the relationship starts to improve, however, friends and family will have more respect for you.

Because there is so much resistance to positive change from family, a very helpful thing to do is to get professional support when you first work on things. This is also one of the reasons that people in coaching make more progress than people who try to make changes on their own, even if they already know what to do. What will also help you get through family resistance is knowing that they will stop resisting once the improvement starts. This can be as short as two to three weeks. Because of the ripple effect, family members will also change to a certain extent. How much will depend on how closely involved they are. People who are in competition with you for your husband's attention are likely to approve at first and then to disapprove later. There never is a way to please everyone.

The Guilt Trap

People often confuse feeling guilty with being responsible, but they are quite different. People can feel guilty for things which they are in fact not responsible (e.g. "If I were a good enough wife, he would treat me nicely"). Guilt is an emotion like any other, and like any other, it has it's purposes. The purpose of guilt is to stop us from doing harmful things to others, which in turn, helps us to get along with others and to get what we need from them. Feeling guilty about what other people do is useless. People with a lot of guilt feelings may make their own lives difficult by putting up too much with others. Even when we have done something wrong, letting others hurt us is wrong. The correct response to guilt is not to let others treat us badly, but to make changes in ourselves that stop harm from being done.

Both men and women are capable of incorrectly responding to guilt, and as a result carry the burden of it much longer than they need to. Guilt which is carried indefinitely benefits no one and adds nothing positive to a relationship. There is no benefit for your spouse if you are a martyr in your relationship. You are part of him and so anything you do to harm yourself (or allow harm to come to yourself), harms him as well. A healthy approach to guilt is to first discover where harm is *continuing* to be done, if at all. Then, to stop it. Thus, if one is having a marital affair, a proper response to guilt would be to stop all activities associated with the affair and instead work productively on building the relationship with one's spouse. If guilt is experienced about something that is *entirely in the past*, then the correct response is forgiveness. Ask forgiveness of others (when appropriate), make amends if possible, and then forgive yourself even if they don't forgive you. There is no need to repeatedly ask others for forgiveness. If you have wronged your husband, then either he will forgive you or he won't. Continuing to do emotional harm to yourself won't help either of you. Letting him treat you badly won't help either of you. Continuing to have a "guilt button" that your husband can push also won't help either of you. If he doesn't' forgive and if he continues to push your "guilt" button, then see this behavior for what it is—attempted manipulation on his part. Then deal with it like the other behaviors in this book. Guilt and forgiveness, when used appropriately, are both marital aids and relationship aids in general. When they are causing harm, then something is wrong.

Irrational Guilt Trap

Can someone feel guilty even if they have stopped the damage and been forgiven? Yes. That is called "irrational guilt." It serves no good purpose because there no longer is any bad behavior. Just as failing to forgive a husband who has really changed his ways is harmful, so is failing to forgive yourself. In other words, irrational guilt is a reluctance to forgive oneself. People in this position will allow others to harm them because they feel that they deserve it. They will allow their husbands to mistreat them and sometimes even wish their husbands would do some bad things to kind of even up the score. Such mental score keeping is very harmful. Forgiveness is supposed to wipe the slate clean—no score, no debt—a new beginning. Failure to forgive yourself is also harmful to your husband because it creates a distance from him which he does not deserve. Also, if because of your guilt you allow him to behave badly toward you, that also damages his relationship with you, and so harms him. There simply is no way to hate yourself while loving your partner and expect good things to happen.

"Failing to Forgive" Trap

The same would be true if you failed to forgive your husband. It would maintain a distance harmful to both of you. As hard as it may be to forgive yourself or your partner, it's what you must do *when the offending behavior is in the past.* Forgiveness before that time will make him lose respect for you.

One theme you will see repeated often in this book is that any harm you allow to come to either you or your husband, harms the relationship. To have a truly good relationship, it must be good for both husband and wife. As the wife, it is your responsibility to help your husband stop doing harm to you. You must also stop doing harm to yourself, for your husband's sake, as well as your own. If you need his help with that, then tell him. That is one of the benefits of marriage. If he doesn't know how to help, you will need to teach him. The number one reason men don't help women with emotional problems is they don't know how. And if you don't know how to help him, you can learn, as you are doing now.

The Insecurity Trap

Yet other women put up with behavior from their difficult husbands for fear of losing them if they don't. There are many women with bad marriages, who choose neither to divorce nor to become a stronger force for their relationship. Ninety-nine percent of the time, it is due to their insecurity. The very same reason that has been around since the 1950's and before. They don't believe they can make it on their own either financially, or emotionally, and so they believe their only option is to stay in a bad relationship. They follow a tradition of mothers "sacrificing" for their children, and children who grow up and think them stupid for not having left their fathers. These women *need* their husbands, even if they don't feel in love with them anymore. For these women, security has become more important than happiness. In days gone by, when it wouldn't have been possible for women to support themselves without a husband, it made sense that women would feel insecure if their husbands were to leave them. Fortunately, now there is a better solution than divorce or being a martyr.

If you allow your husband to mistreat you in any way, you lose your husband's respect. Because it's hard to love someone you don't respect, it puts the relationship at risk for both you and your husband. This is not to say that you are responsible for your husband's behavior—far from it—he is responsible for his own behavior. But, you are responsible for how you respond to his behavior—particularly when that behavior is ongoing. Hurt me once, shame on you; hurt me twice, shame on me. Hurt me over and over again while I allow you to is insanely wrong. Relationships are not meant to be never ending nightmares. They are not a good way to deal with your insecurity.

Escaping the Insecurity Trap by Overcoming Neediness

The first way out of this trap is to become less needy so you have the *ability* to survive and thrive without your husband. Knowing you are capable of living well without your husband will bring the temptation to leave. But it also will allow you to do what is really needed to save your relationship—to demand and get respect, and to relate to each other on an equal basis. Equality in a relationship is about trust, respect, and love. The clear message that needs to be given in both words and actions are, "I will listen to you and love you, but you will talk nicely and listen to me." A needy person is always subordinate to her partner. A person who is not needy is in the position to be a good partner.

If you hate the way your relationship is, but find yourself paralyzed and unable to either get out of it or do anything about it, then now is the time to realize what is really making you stuck. It is your own neediness. Let me be clear about this and say again that you are *not* causing the problems in your relationship. Very likely, your husband is. But, your neediness is stopping you from doing anything about it.

Neediness is actually not as bad as it sounds. Everybody needs things both emotional and physical. It is part of being human. We are not machines nor would any person want to marry one. We all need love, attention, affection, food, heat, shelter, etc. But, when your needs are being met *primarily* by your husband, and you have no way to get them met otherwise, it puts you in a one down position from him. We don't want your husband to feel unneeded. But, we don't want him to feel like he can control or own you, either. We want him to feel like you desire him very much, but that you *could* live without him.

You may realize this about your relationships at work—you are a viable and desirable employee. Your coworkers like you. But, they could all get along without you. Knowing this really helps you not to just cut loose with your feelings, doesn't it? They like you and want you, but could do without you. It is only at this equal level that *partnership* can happen. Otherwise, you will be parenting him, or he will be parenting you. That's not what marriage is all about. I regularly help people to strengthen their marriage by helping them to share more and need less. For some people, this means making friends, becoming more active outside of home, or getting job skills. For others, it is learning to bolster their self-esteem, discover their dreams, and go for it. Not only do people become less needy when they do these things, they become more *interesting*. They have things to talk about. They have people to talk to. And, they have things to do. So, they have a lot to share. Good talking can't happen without something to talk about. Overcoming neediness makes people less dependent on their partners, but gives them more to share with their partners. And less fear when they do share. The less you *need* your husband, the more free you will feel to truly love him without fear. And, the easier it will be for you to make the kind of changes that will help him to change—like setting good boundaries. A needy person with a kind, gentle, and easy going partner may do alright. But, a needy person with an overbearing, difficult, withdrawn, manipulative, or insecure partner will have problems. For women with difficult husbands, neediness must go if they are to improve their marriage.

If a difficult man dates a very secure woman, how long do you think she will allow him to mistreat her? One time? Maybe. Two? No way. After the first time he would quickly get the message that he needs to be nice to her to keep her and their relationship would have a very good chance. She would probably make it very clear what is acceptable to her and what is not. And then, he could take it or leave it, but he couldn't mistreat her anymore.

Your relationship with your husband can also have that very good chance when *you* become that secure (loving, not mean) woman and when you earn your husband's respect. As long as you fear losing him, you take away any fear he has of losing you. And just like children, we need to know that if we don't treat our friends well, they will no longer play with us, and will no longer be our friends. That protects a friendship. It doesn't end it. You can have that same kind of protection when you overcome your insecurities and your neediness. Overcoming your fears and insecurities will be the beginning of a better relationship with your husband and a better life for yourself.

The Fatigue Trap

Some women put up with difficult behavior from their husbands because they are too tired or exhausted to do anything else. Human beings only have a certain amount of physical and emotional energy. When pushed beyond that limit, our emotions shut down, and our bodies can do no more. Although very few people in modern countries ever get to the point where they literally can't do anything more, they do get to the point where they have no *desire* to do anything more. That lack of desire is actually one of our defense mechanisms at work. The lack of desire prevents us from taking on more obligations, allowing us to rest and recover. The word used to describe this continuous low energy, low desire condition is "burnout." A burned-out bulb doesn't shine at all. A burned-out person "shines" dimly—just enough to get by. How brightly are you shining?

When women get to the point of burnout, they no longer feel love for their husbands. In fact, they may not feel love for anyone, their emotions having been virtually shut off. The burnout can result from dealing with chronically bad behavior from their husbands, but it can result from many other causes as well, including overwork, lack of sleep, chronic medical conditions, and certain psychological disorders (especially of the anxious type which keep the mind and body racing). Many relationships exist at a kind of marginal level where people don't feel love for each other and they don't feel hate either. A couple can just "exist" or continue without really knowing why. This is burnout in a relationship

A key characteristic of burnout in these situations is that women don't do anything to change their situation—whether it is to end the relationship or try to improve it. It has been my clinical experience that emotions return (both good and bad) when a person is able to rest and recover from burnout. Before that happens, even the best plan in the world will not be followed because the woman (or man) simply does not have enough energy or the desire do what needs to be done. They can still see rationally what a good plan would be, but they just don't have the will or energy to do it.

What I most want you to know if you are on your way to burnout (if you were already there, you wouldn't have the energy to read this book) is that your lack of love for your husband (or he for you) is not permanently gone. Because of chronic fatigue from other factors and/or stress from your marriage, your emotions have been switched off or turned down to "low." They have not gone away. If I turn out the lights in my room at night, there are many things that I can't see. They haven't disappeared. They are still there. If I turn the light on again, I will be able to see them again—just as well as before. Recover from the burnout, and the feelings come right back. If your husband is burned out, the same is true for him.

If you are feeling like you would like to give up, it's likely you are just getting burned out trying something that doesn't work. It's like eating tomato soup with a fork—you get a taste, but never get filled up. If you continue in the same way, you will eventually give up, because you will have even less desire than you do now. The best thing would be for you to follow the feeling to give up, but not on the relationship. Rather give up the *method* you are using to work on the relationship. It is that method that is not working. It is the ineffectiveness of that method that is burning you out and switching off your loving feelings. As soon as you and your husband discover and use effective methods to build your relationship, the positive feelings will begin to return. Let me say that again—your lack of love is connected with the overuse of ineffective methods. Like running on a treadmill, they get you nowhere. And the more you use them, the faster you burnout. Get off the treadmill and then you can really go somewhere. As soon as you make progress, your feelings of love will return. This is true for people who are feeling burned out and hopeless in *any* situation. Repeated, ineffective actions lead to burnout, and repeated, effective actions lead to success.

Sometimes it helps us to see better if we consider the same problem from another angle. To give you just one example, consider school children who, despite working very hard, continue to receive bad grades. After a while, what happens? They no longer try, nor do they feel like trying. You can make them work, but their heart won't be in it and their grades won't improve. The solution for them is not to drop out of school anymore than it is for you to end your relationship. The solution for them is to start to have some success getting good grades. The only way they are going to be able to do that is by learning to take notes, study, and take tests in a different way. Probably with extra help, like tutoring. Those are the core tasks that will lead to success if done correctly and consistently. Solving relationship problems like yours doesn't mean working harder. It means getting more help to learn effective actions and then taking them until you get change.

I know that you have the ability to learn new and better ways of doing things. But first you need to see what is not working and be willing to give it up. Not your relationship—just your current approach. Let go of the fork, so you can pick up the spoon and get more out of your relationship. New methods will bring you success and encourage you to keep on having success in your marriage. Then the fires of love will re-ignite between you and your husband.

Religious Confusion Trap

Some women, believe that it is their moral or religious *duty* to allow their husband to continue their bad behavior. Of course, they don't think of it that way. They believe that God hates divorce and conclude that whatever doesn't result in divorce is right. While I agree that divorce is a terrible thing to be avoided, so are many other things in a relationship. Like abuse, disrespect, and emotional neglect. Avoiding one bad thing (divorce) just to do another (have a bad relationship) doesn't make sense to me. There are other choices much better than these. Love is "patient and kind," as the Bible says (1 Corinthians 13:4a), but it is not patient and kind to allow your husband to continue to do things which hurt you and him, any more than it would be patient and kind to let your child be a bully or play on a busy street.

It is precisely because love is patient and kind that we need to help our spouses to have good relationships with us. We do it patiently, which means without giving up, with the best of intentions for the welfare of our partner. One of the *least* loving things we can do is to let them continue to do harm to us, because it harms them, too. There is no good that can come to your husband by allowing him to continue to behave badly toward you. You can test this by asking yourself, "What is best for the long term welfare of my husband?—to allow him to continue to mistreat me? Or to help him to stop and have a better relationship with me?"

We discipline our children not because we wish to hurt them, get revenge, or because they deserve it, but because they need to learn the best way to get along. To do nothing when they are doing wrong would truly be harmful. The same principle holds for our spouses, our neighbors, and for international politics. We stop evil. We don't return evil for evil. Our motivation must always be in the best interest of the other person. This means that sometimes we must give the person the opposite of what they actually want because it is what is best for them. Sometimes we too have to take some awful tasting medicine when it truly helps.

Love Is the Highest Principle

As a loving person, your motivation must never be to hurt your husband, but in the process of loving your husband some of the things you do may make him feel hurt. Just because he feels hurt, doesn't mean you have done something wrong to him. Also, you may at times feel hurt, when he tells you what you need to hear. Even a fool sometimes says wise things. For my clients, I warn them that I won't always tell them what they want to hear, but I will always tell them what I think will help them. Because my help shows them how much I care, they usually take my feedback really well.

Summary

Perhaps you were able to see some elements of yourself in the descriptions in this chapter and other things that didn't quite fit. That is necessarily so, for no one can be clearly defined. The earth is a world of seven billion individuals. One reason for that is that we are all in a state of change. How we were as children does not match how we are now, and how we are now will not match the way we will become.

Change is inevitable, but good change is not. For that, we must make as many good decisions as possible and then act boldly on them. Such is your case now, with your difficult partner. Whatever has been keeping you from changing things has not really been the right thing even if it feels right. And your actions or inactions are harming you as much as anyone else. What you have been doing probably helps you to feel more secure, but in reality, there is no way to have total security—whether you are single or married, rich or poor, passive or confrontational. We are always putting something at risk. When we risk for love, at least we are risking for something we believe in. We do our best, and we have faith that no matter what happens, we will be alright and that life will still somehow go on.

There have been times in my life when I knew that if I didn't take action, that I would lose my chance. For example, when I decided to give up my established psychology practice and move to Japan to marry my wife. I knew that if I didn't make that move, that I never would. And what I had to lose by not moving was greater than what I could keep by staying. Because, although I could practice psychology in other places, there was only one Toshie, who I loved with all my heart. I hope that you feel or remember those feelings about your husband and that you honor the sacrifices you have made by making the best relationship you possibly can now. It can be done, but not by sheer force of will alone. That way leads to burnout. It must be done by being smart and by being persistent. In the coming pages, I will give you effective methods to help you do both of those things.

6

TEN GOOD REASONS TO HELP HIM CHANGE

Why even think about helping your husband? Why should you do anything to help your husband if he is so difficult? Here are four good reasons to start: (1) Because you love him (even if you don't feel it right now), (2) because of your history together, (3) because you don't like to think of yourself as a quitter, and (4) if you can really help your husband to change his problem behavior, you know that you can enjoy your relationship with him. If you need to leave him, you can, any time you wish. But this is the only time you have left to make things better. And, if it's possible to make things better, aren't you willing to do whatever you have to do?

Your husband has already committed his life to you, and to recapture his heart is worth a little extra work. Everything you do to build your relationship will help both of you. A relationship always involves two people, after all. You can cut him out of your life, but not without cutting yourself too. Let's not do that if it isn't necessary.

If your husband did not want a relationship with you for some reason, he would not be in a relationship with you. He would leave you immediately. There is *some reason* why he is staying in the relationship with you. Remember that the next time you wonder if he needs you. He needs you for *something*. And, that is something that you both have in common. Because you have stayed with him for some reason.

If you were doing something that was really destructive to your relationship, you would want him to help you stop it, wouldn't you? What would it mean if he wasn't concerned about you stopping? Or did nothing to help you change if he could? Failing to help, when we can, does as much harm as whatever our partner does. It is not our obligation in a legal sense, but it is part of what we mean when we commit our love to someone. We do what we can to help. If we are then rejected, we let them go. Love doesn't force, but it does help.

Well, in case this introduction and the first four reasons didn't convince you, the following are six more reasons to help your husband to have a better relationship with you now.

Reason Five: Better Social Relationships

In the process of learning how to help your husband (to overcome his difficult behaviors with you), you will also be learning how to manage other men *and* women in your life. The skills don't apply only to your husband. Have an overbearing mom? A withdrawn friend? A demanding boss? You will find that the techniques that work with your husband also work with others—to the extent that they are motivated to have a relationship with you (as a daughter, employee, friend, etc.). If they are not yet motivated to have a relationship with you, then you will need to create that desire in them before you will be able to have any positive influence over them. There are ways to do that, too.

Reason Six: To Help Your Husband (and Yourself) to Have a Good Reputation

Who cares what other people think? Anyone who relies on other people for their income, their children's education, and their socialization, among others. Everything meaningful that we want to accomplish in life is connected with other people. We need their good will and cooperation. No matter how you feel about former President Bill Clinton, you have to admire his wife for not damaging both of their reputations by seeking some sort of revenge for her husband's infidelity. Many people could have understood revenge, but it would have cost both of them more than they wanted to lose.

Doing nothing can also harm your reputation. When your husband treats you badly, whose reputation does that hurt? Both of you, right? It hurts his reputation for being a man who treats women that way, especially his wife, and you also get a bad reputation for being a woman who puts up with such behavior. Being mistreated by your husband will get you some sympathy face-to-face, but a lot of gossip behind your back. Much of what people say will be their guesses, or attempts to make sense out of why such things are happening in your relationship. Whatever they guess, it's not going to be good. Your children, if you have any, are also not going to want to talk about your family situation with friends and may be very careful about bringing friends home. They don't want the bad reputation of their parents to rub off on them. Their acceptance or lack of acceptance by their peer group may be much harder to deal with than what you have to face as an adult.

Overreacting and under reacting are clearly not the ways to go if you want to preserve your reputation. The middle road approach is to stop his difficult behavior, and earn his respect with good boundaries. When you do that, your reputation will improve. When he then chooses to earn your trust, his reputation will improve as well. You will not get an immediate increase in reputation, but it will gradually build. Learning how to handle your husband's bad behavior in public situations will also preserve public respect.

Reason Seven: To Have Better Money Management

Conflicts about money burn out more relationships than any other topic. Money problems are a reality which cannot be ignored. Overspending or mismanagement of funds will cause repeated conflict until the problem is resolved or the marriage is over. The way we handle money is also connected to many emotional issues and values, such as what we think is important to spend money on, whose money it is, and who gets to determine how the money is spent. Because much of the conflict about money is emotional, the answer for couples is to learn money management *and* to find a way to communicate and cooperate about their values and needs. When you have an uncooperative husband, that is a very difficult thing to do. Some husbands won't talk, some won't listen, and some won't do either.

As you improve your relationship with your husband you will both be able to communicate better about everything, including money. Add on top of that some financial skills and you and your husband can reverse a bad financial and emotional trend in your relationship. In a way, improving your relationship with your difficult man can be like putting money in the bank.

Reason Eight: Make Your Kids Happier

Kids are affected at a deep emotional level by the kind of relationship their parents have with each other. Even when both parents have a good relationship with their children, marital stress will impact the way the children relate to their future spouses. Can't they simply do the opposite of what you and your husband do? Or won't they be more careful to choose a better partner? Although they may try to do that, they won't be able to judge what a healthy partner is or what a healthy relationship is. There are a hundred kinds of bad relationships, so avoiding your mistakes doesn't mean they will necessarily have a good relationship.

Relationship skills are not taught at school, and even if they were, they wouldn't do much for future relationships. What *you do* will be remembered. Girls can learn from you healthy and loving ways to deal with difficult men. Boys will learn why it is helpful for men to respect women. If you don't have children, it is still helpful for you to imagine that you have an adult daughter who has a relationship just like yours. How would you want her to handle it? Would you want her to quickly divorce? To just be patient year after year? To learn to set limits while still being loving? Hopefully, you would want for her the latter. Whatever you would want for your daughter should be the same as what you now want for yourself.

Reason Nine: Boost Your Self-Esteem

Self-esteem is one of those mystical terms that we can simplify here to mean "like yourself better." When you deal effectively with problems—any problems—you like yourself better. And when you like yourself, you feel more competent and have more success. When you can handle more than before, things that used to stress you a lot will stress you less. Whatever your husband does that you don't like, will stress you less when you know how to deal with it. Those buttons that he pushes are the things that you need to work on.

Good self-esteem does not start the minute you start working on your relationship. Here's why. At first, when you learn new ways to deal with old problems, they will seem strange to you, because you have never done things that way before. Rather than being confident, you will be skeptical and doubt yourself. It may even feel like your first time on the high diving board. As you continue to use the new ways and begin to experience success with them, they will feel less and less strange. As you further continue to use them and have more and more success, they will become your new habits. They will be part of who you are (a more assertive person, for example). This is how confidence develops, like when you learn a new language. At first, the new words are foreign and unfamiliar. Then you feel hesitant and awkward when you first use them. After you get good at saying them, they become easy and natural. And you enjoy using them.

You may have experienced this process in reverse (creating low self-esteem) if you got used to doing things in a bad way in your relationship. At first, you were upset by your own bad reactions (fighting or withdrawing, for example). Then, you gradually got used to being that way. Now, it may feel more comfortable to avoid your husband than to talk to him. Because you aren't experiencing success, though, you feel miserable. As a result, you like your "new" self less than the old one. And it is easier to be stressed by things that didn't bother you before. You become sensitized to anything which reminds you of what you hate.

When you work on relationship skills, you transform into a person you like and respect better. That is what self-esteem is all about.

Now, let's consider your husband's perception of your changes. As you change the way you do things with him, or the way you respond to him, he will, grudgingly, have to change the way he interacts with you. For example, if you are walking away whenever he shouts, he will either need to learn not to shout or get used to shouting all by himself. At first, that will be a very uncomfortable thing for him. He won't be used to that and it won't feel natural for him. He will resist it, no matter how much better that new way is. He will think you are making things worse. That will be the toughest time for you. If you understand the process, though, you will realize that his resistance is actually part of the process of change. You and he will be going through the early learning stage where things feel uncomfortable. It will shake things up a little. As you both get used to it, things will settle down and be better than before. In essence, you will have helped him to improve his self-esteem by helping him to behave better towards you! That will make him feel more like an effective man—something that is important for all men's self-esteem. (By the way, walking away is only one part of one possible intervention).

Reason Ten: To Have Greater Family Harmony— Maybe

It really is unlikely that both of your families (families of origin) are healthy and that your relationship just happens to be messed up. People with messed up relationships almost always come from families that are messed up. When you work on changing the way you relate to your husband, it will have a ripple effect on other people. People living with you will be impacted the most. Nowadays, that is likely to be children only, though some people have multigenerational homes (mine is three generations, two different cultures, and three different religions!).

So don't expect people to be on your side right away. Most people in your family and your husband's will not be supportive of your making any changes. The main reason? Just like your husband—they are used to the way things are, even if things are not that good. Since you have not shown yourself to be an effective positive change agent up to this point, they have little confidence in your being one now. The results of your changes are unknown and they don't have the big picture. People fear the unknown. The present situation may be bad, but at least they know what to expect. Start making changes and they will fear that things are going to become even worse. It's *that fearful image* that they react to and not what you are doing. They will either get angry with you, think you are crazy, or both, depending on what they imagine will happen.

The fear of change influences people to live unhappy lives rather than take a chance on making things even worse. Does that make sense? Certainly not from a logical perspective, but it does from an emotional one. People decide with their emotions first and then justify with their reasons. What this means is that when you start to change things in your home, the level of tension in your family will rise. And you know how each person in your family deals with tension. I am not saying these things to discourage you. I am saying them to help you realize that your family's discomfort will actually be a sign of progress! It's an early stage indicator that you are making necessary changes. Every change initially creates tension before it produces results. A sprinter must push backwards so she can move forwards. That first push takes a mighty effort. But once she gets moving, it is easier to stay moving.

Everybody who starts a new job or new school or moves to a new area goes through tension on the way to adjustment, growth, and a better way of life. In fact, if there is no tension in your home when you start to work on things, that probably means that nothing really is changing. You may have made changes in your head, but they haven't become visible in your interactions yet. Remember those ripples of influence that I talked about? Those ripples will first hit your husband, then your children, and then your families of origin.

Your husband's parents in particular are most likely to side with him against you because what they see you doing won't make sense to them (your husband was produced in their mould). The tension they experience will be part of their own positive change. It is a necessary and healthy reaction on their part, although quite a nuisance to you. It will decrease once everyone starts getting used to the better relationship you create. And, although your in-laws may be a little more leery of you, they will respect you more, too. Your husband will still interact with them the way he always has, so they will also be reassured by that.

The bottom line is when you improve your relationship with your husband, you will improve life for your immediate family, but only after they adjust to the changes. They are not likely to give you credit, but you can learn to pat yourself on the back (the quickest and easiest way to get a pat on the back). If you are working with a coach or counselor, he or she will tell you "well done."

Summary

Change is difficult, but worthwhile. Without change, we would all still behave like infants. Change is a process. We learn new things, and we feel awkward at first. We keep doing them until we become comfortable with them. Change is the way we grow. There are at least 10 reasons to intentionally go through this change process with your husband.

The only alternative to change is to not change, and you know where that will lead you.

7

REDUCING THE RISK OF VIOLENCE

This book is not for people who are in physical danger.

This book was written to give women hope in relationships where it seems like nothing can change, and to also provide practical steps that women can take to make significant improvement before considering divorce. It does not address the interventions required for men who are violent, have been violent in the past, or who have threatened violence. Women and men in such relationships need help, but because of the amount of risk involved, those interventions are best done with the help and protection of specialists and law enforcement. Some men, under the right conditions, will injure or even kill their partners, their children and/or themselves. Although not the norm, it happens enough that every woman needs to be aware of this possibility.

The previous paragraph is as far as many authors go, but I want to take it a step further. Violence is a reality that can happen with any partner whether it has happened before or not. For most people, including myself, it is a reasonable risk to have a partner, because we judge the possible rewards to outweigh the possible risks. Because we don't have a crystal ball which tells the future (and who would really want one?), we need to make choices that match our best hopes and dreams but also prepare for things that could go wrong.

This chapter is about both prevention of violence and preparation for that possibility. It is not about stopping violence. It is most useful for women who don't expect violence but who need to prepare. Preparing is also a kind of prevention.

The interventions in this book are less risky than telling your husband you are divorcing or ending the relationship. Like all interventions, they initially increase stress, which is why you shouldn't do them with men who already physically explode all too easily. There is no safety however, in avoiding working on a problem relationship. Marriage problems cause ongoing stress, and too often a wasted relationship filled with anger and regret. Because your situation is unique, and because I don't know you or your partner, I cannot weigh the risks or make the decisions for you. You must decide on your own whether to work on your relationship. If you decide to, then you must also decide whether to get professional help or not. In all cases where violence or threats of violence are an issue, or become an issue, professional help should be sought.

Feeling Safe Is a Requirement for Intervention

You will not be able to get to a place where you can feel secure, talk honestly, and set good boundaries as long as you feel you or your children are at risk of injury. As a child I saw the effects of such insecurity on a marriage, first hand. I know the terrible stress children are under when they fear that they or their mother could be hurt by her husband. Even when he does not hit, the stress is there.

So, my first rule for you is whether or not you currently feel endangered, if there has been violence or threats of violence, do your interventions with professional help from the start. And in the meantime, do whatever you need to do to keep you and your children safe. The police are for emergencies, the courthouse for protection from abuse (PFA) orders, a local counselor (preferably PhD, PsyD, or DMFT level) for guidance, friends or a women's shelter for protection, and also national abuse hotline numbers for emergency guidance.[5] Protecting yourself helps your partner as well. Anything that he does to hurt you, harms your relationship, harms his self-respect, reduces other people's respect for him, and has possible criminal repercussions.

Many women who are abused physically or who are with potentially violent men choose not to end their relationship. Women who stay in such relationships often believe that the benefits of the relationship are worth the risk. Whether that is a good decision or not, it is a reality and professionals need to have a better answer for such women than "Run for the hills and forget that man!" Women need to be taught how to stay safe and not simply told to leave their partner. There is nothing simple or safe about leaving a partner, violent or otherwise.

Everyone Reacts Negatively to Change at First

Why would trying to improve your marriage initially increase stress and the risk of violence? The main reason is because the violence of another person (such as your partner) is not connected to your motivations. People react to what you say and do, not to what you are thinking, feeling, or intending. While you are making changes that are necessary to have a better relationship, they are reacting to their fears about change. They automatically imagine the worst possible outcome of those changes, and then react emotionally to that image. This happens largely at a subconscious level. In the blink of an eye.

Without change, people feel secure with the way things are (even if they are unhappy) because they know what tomorrow is going to be like and the day after that and the day after that. People's need to feel secure is stronger than their desire to be happy. When you introduce a change, they no longer know what is going to happen. They become instantly insecure and stressed. Even though you are

---

[5] In the United States call 1-800-799-SAFE, or go to www.thehotline.org; for other countries check your telephone directory, directory assistance, or web search engine.

working on making tomorrow a better day for you and your partner, and explain that, your partner only sees that as one possibility among others that he thinks are more likely. He won't start to imagine things can actually be better until after he sees it happen. The time span between your intervention and his seeing improvement is where the danger is. No matter how small of a change you make or how lovingly you communicate, there will always be a time of stress—a time of uncertainty where anything is possible.

Stress and adjustment happen in our lives all the time—not just with relationship interventions. For example, if there is a change in the way we are expected to submit paperwork for our jobs, we don't immediately imagine its benefits. Instead, we groan about it being another thing we have to deal with and about how it's probably going to make our jobs more difficult and frustrating. It's the rare person who immediately thinks, "They changed the way I need to do paperwork. Maybe it will be easier, more efficient, and make my life more enjoyable!" When the government raises taxes, it causes outrage at first because people imagine having even more difficulty paying their bills. Can you imagine someone thinking, "They raised my taxes. That's probably going to result in a better run country and a better way of life for all of us. I'm looking forward to the improvements"? Reacting positively to changes that we perceive as negative seems crazy. It's normal for your husband to react negatively when your relationship is already distressed.

If you had the kind of husband who thought, "Oh boy, she's changing the way we do things. I'm really looking forward to the increased closeness it will bring," then you would not be reading this book. Even men who are not difficult don't have this kind of reaction to change. There is no sense in looking for a stress-free way to make changes with a difficult husband—it doesn't exist. Besides, if he had no reaction at all, the intervention would not be effective.

Change is the Process of Adapting To Stress

Change creates stress because: 1) of what it makes people imagine; 2) it reminds them of changes for the worse that happened in the past; and 3) it requires extra effort. The greater the perceived effort, the greater the stress. For example, imagining a more attractive figure motivates us to diet and exercise but the anticipated difficulty stops most people from even trying. Some people are motivated enough to try but then are stopped by actual difficulty. It takes a strong belief in oneself and/or extra support to continue until success results. When we persevere despite the stress, it brings adjustment and success.

People's ability to tolerate stress and adapt to change (to persevere) depends on both their physical and mental health. If you worked on the 10th floor of a building and the elevator broke down, how much would that stress you? It probably depends on how good your physical condition is. If you are a marathoner, you may already use the stairs, so it wouldn't stress you at all. You might enjoy running up the stairs past your puffing coworkers. But, if you are in poor physical condition, it could ruin your day and make you dread going to work the next day. You could fear having a heart attack or you could aggravate an existing medical condition.

The type of men this book is about are not in good emotional shape. They are emotional elevator riders and donut eaters. They do what makes them feel good in the short-term even if their relationships suffer in the long term. They might think that they "should" improve, but the anticipated difficulty of doing that prevents them. When you do an intervention, their emotional "elevator" breaks down. You introduce a change which they have to adjust to.

In the example of the broken down work elevator, what would happen if the elevator didn't get fixed? A few people might quit their job, particularly if they had a better offer elsewhere. But, that would be true even if the elevator wasn't broken down. Most people, though, would not only get used to taking the stairs, after a while they would actually get in better physical shape. They would stop fighting about it and just accept it as part of the job. They may even start to brag about it to others as they get in better condition. Likewise, when changes happen in amounts that are not beyond a husband's ability to cope, he adjusts. This is the process we use for interventions to help our partners to change in positive ways. You make his emotional elevator (usually powered by your codependence) break down. As a result, he gets into better emotional and relational "shape."

Avoiding His Stress Ceiling

For a moment, let's imagine that you didn't work on the 10th floor, but you worked on the 100th floor. If the elevator broke down, you might refuse to work at all regardless of how much you needed the job. Or you might try to climb the stairs, but give up before you could reach the top. If you did manage to reach the top, you might be so sore and upset about it that you just couldn't imagine working another day like that.

In this extreme stress situation, adjustment wouldn't happen. Instead, breakdown would happen. When stress is beyond a person's physical and/or emotional ability to adjust, the body and mind break down. Physically, this means stress injuries. Emotionally, this means psychological disorders, social withdrawal, and an intensification of previous coping responses. People who cope by avoidance avoid more, people who cope with anger become more angry. The interventions you do need to be well below your partner's stress ceiling.

If your husband feels that a change is beyond his ability to deal with, he can behave in extreme ways. He could become violent against himself and/or others. Even if he has never been violent before, there is a first time for everything. Because stress is additive, if your husband is already stressed before your intervention, even a small intervention may bring him to his stress ceiling. A cup that is completely full can't hold even one more drop.

A Graduated Approach is Less Stressful

The interventions in this book are designed to not create a 100th floor kind of experience. The changes you will make are small at first, which allows you to see how your husband reacts. It is always good to test the depth of the water before diving in. Women who suddenly do drastic interventions, like tell their husband they are leaving them because they can't stand them anymore, are doing a much more drastic thing than what these interventions do. I help women to minimize drastic reactions from their partners by teaching them to do non-rejecting, non-confrontational, graduated interventions.

A Non-Rejecting Approach

The "I can't stand you; I'm divorcing you," message is very rejecting as well as stressful. It kicks open emotional doors that may be locked deep in your husband's mind. Such a statement will trigger feelings he had when he felt rejected or worthless before. It can bring great despair and great anger at the same time—a dangerous and even deadly combination. Men who come to me for help at such a time are often in a panic state. They have to be calmed down for a while before they can think about making positive changes.

On the other hand, the interventions in this book are always accompanied by the sincere message, "I love you and want our relationship to be better." This is sincere, otherwise you could not do these interventions. It is a very important part of the interventions to say this because it influences the way your husband interprets your behavior. It also touches on what he wants. Because unless he no longer wants a relationship with you, he also wants a good relationship with you. No one wants to have a bad relationship.

Keeping Safe: Preparation Is Better Than Reacting

Knowing what to do to avoid getting hurt is even more important than knowing what to do after you get hurt. Preventing a fire is better than a dozen fire trucks. Your number one strategy for keeping safe should be to avoid danger. But this does not mean living as a timid person, walking on eggshells, lest you upset your husband. If your husband is so dangerous you need to live in fear, leave your home, go to a safe place, don't tell your husband where you are, and get professional help. This is by no means running away from your relationship. It is taking positive steps to save it. Waiting until you are hurt to take action would make it more difficult to restore your relationship.

If you are not in this situation, but sense danger when interacting with your husband, back down. Don't escalate the situation. Don't confront him about it. Get help without telling your husband first. Men are usually upset when their wives tell them they are not feeling safe and that they're getting help. This is one secret you need to temporarily have for the sake of yourself and your relationship.

The self-help interventions in this book are for women who believe their husband's behavior threatens their relationship, not their physical safety. If the going gets too difficult or if you sense danger, then get professional help before proceeding further.

If There Has Been Past Violence or Threats of Violence

If your husband has ever been violent towards you or another partner, it is in his repertoire of coping responses. No matter how much he may regret it, it still has some place among the reactions he could have. People always have to cope in some way, even if it is in a bad way. When people are upset, they don't think rationally and do things they regret later. They do what comes most easily, even if it has bad consequences. This means that if your husband has often used violence when frustrated, it is highly likely that it will happen again. If he has rarely used violence, other responses are more likely, but violence is still possible, particularly if his stress level is high.

The interventions in this book have safeguards designed to limit the extreme stress which would increase the risk of violence. Specifically, by avoiding arguing, by agreeing with your husband on ideas you have in common, and by not taking sudden or drastic actions, stress is less than with more confrontational methods. Be sure that you do the interventions without arguing or threats. If at any time you believe taking an action or saying something would create a dangerous situation for you or others, don't say it or do it without professional help.

If threatened, back down, get away, and get help. If you don't back down in the face of a threat, you may be hurt or even killed. If you back down, but do nothing else, you will be respected even less than before, your husband's threat response will be rewarded, and you are even more likely to be threatened or hurt in the future. If you back down and get help dealing with him, you will be safer (though there is no way to eliminate risk no matter what you do), and you will be able to take effective action to make it clear to him that threats will harm his relationship with you and put his whole future at risk.

If you are intending to improve your relationship, consider carefully before telling your family or friends about your husband's threats, unless it is part of an intervention you are doing with a professional or unless you have no other help. Telling your friends or family may put them at risk, and will certainly prejudice them against your husband. If you were divorcing, that might not be so bad, but if you are working on helping your husband to overcome his problem and to make your relationship better, it will be one more obstacle that will get in the way.

If There Is an Increase in Substance Abuse

If your husband chooses to cope with the stress of adjustment by drinking more alcohol or abusing other drugs, then you should stop your intervention. The intervention you will need to use is one for substance abuse. Although it may not seem to be a problem most of the time, its use stands in the way of your relationship improving. A man who needs drugs or alcohol to cope (not including the legitimate use of prescription medication), is a man with a drug or alcohol problem, or more specifically, a coping problem.

Other problems related to increased substance abuse are impaired judgment and reduced inhibition. Normally we all have temptations at times to do things which are socially inappropriate and/or harmful. We inhibit or stop such behaviors because of the consequences it would bring to ourselves and to others. We are generally careful not to behave differently from the way we usually do unless we have a very good reason. However, under the influence of drugs or alcohol we may see clearly what we are doing but have less concern for the consequences of what we are doing. A man who would never hurt you sober may hurt you when he is drunk or drugged.

It is foolish to argue with a drunk or substance abuser. It is just as foolish to reason with one. Abusing drugs or alcohol is not a reasonable thing. It is an emotional and biological thing. Use your reasoning to keep yourself at a safe distance and to get professional help to know the best way to deal with your partner. Interventions for substance abuse need to come before the interventions in this book. A good place to start to learn about interventions with an alcohol abusing husband is with Al-Anon[6] and with a drug abusing husband is with Nar-Anon.[7]

The interventions in this book will be helpful once the substance abuse problem is dealt with because removing an addiction does not automatically solve other problems. But solving other problems will help the reformed substance abuser not to relapse. This is because he will learn to cope by dealing with his problems rather than drowning them out or by dulling his feelings. Also, he will have your support to help him stay strong. The interventions in this book encourage you to love and support your husband, even when you need to reject his behavior.

Don't Threaten Your Husband

Threatening anyone increases the risk of violence from that person and also increases the chances of him doing self harm. When frightened, humans are not so different from animals. Most animals, when overpowered, will surrender and back off. But when they feel trapped and cannot escape, they will fight. When unable to fight or escape, they become erratic and unpredictable.

---

[6] www.al-anon.alateen.org
[7] www.nar-anon.org

Throughout this book I discourage women from threatening separation or divorce. Instead, I encourage positive, clear, and honest communication. We make sure there is always a way for your husband to improve his relationship with you. If he prefers to end the relationship in favor of his behaviors, he also has that choice. He doesn't need to feel trapped. He is never given a position without options and you agree to help him either way.

The more choices you can give someone, the less likely they are to become violent. The choices help them to be rational because considering choices is a rational process. So, saying, "You have to do X or else," will trap your husband and increase his irrational behavior. Instead saying, "You can do X. or Y, and whichever one you choose, I will help you with," not only keeps him from feeling trapped, it also puts you both on the same side—as allies. That brings the continued possibility of emotionally reconnecting. You sure can't fight your way to a better relationship.

Threats to separate or divorce can easily make a man feel trapped—like he has no choice. In such a situation he may surrender. Or he may attack. Or he may surrender for the moment and attack later. Partnership, and not threats are the way to promote your relationship and minimize stress.

Don't Escalate Arguments

When reading the interventions in this book, you will notice that there is never a place for arguing. Almost all of the couples that I have worked with have argued in their relationship (though some people never argue). Of those that did, they have reported that arguing sometimes resulted in their getting their way or in their partner getting their way, but they have never reported arguing as improving their relationship. On the contrary, they have all reported that arguing makes their relationship more distant, even when they get what they want.

One of the ways to remain close is to not argue. But, the other extreme of avoiding conflict, shutting up, and shutting down, is also harmful to a relationship. The approach I recommend and teach is based on finding common ground, even in the midst of differences, and building on that. Even if one partner wants a divorce and one partner doesn't, neither wants a bad relationship and that is where we start.

Even when a husband has an affair, mortgages the home to pay his gambling bill, or does other such shocking things, rebuilding will only happen from common ground. If a woman wants to leave her husband at these times, I won't blame her for it. But, if she wants to work through it and improve her relationship, as well as reduce the likelihood that such a thing could happen again, we need to start from common ground. I also need to help her to have good boundaries and give her safe ways to express all the hurt and rage that she feels. Working with the idea of common ground helps with all of these things.

The embedded messages in arguments are "You are stupid," "You are bad," and/or "You are wrong." These messages come across loud and clear even when they are not spoken and create defensive or counterattacking reactions. Many people will remember getting such messages from their partner or their parents, but probably no one will ever say that it was a good message or a helpful one. Not only should you not argue with a violent man, or a threatening man, you shouldn't argue with anybody. Instead, with your husband at least, the message which comes out of the lips much less easily needs to be, "I love you," "You are important to me," "I am looking forward to our future together," coupled with your concerns as well as any boundaries that you need to put in place to make sure the relationship stays good. Some defensiveness and counterattacks will still happen, but when you persist in finding common ground and affirming your partner, damage is reduced and fear (and the anger that protects people from self-blaming) is reduced. "I love you son and I don't want anything to happen to you, so I can't let you X," may still get a very angry response from a son, but as long as your actions are reasonable, in the long run it won't damage the relationship. "I love you honey, and I don't want anything to happen to our relationship, so I'm not going to just sit around the house waiting every night for you to come home after midnight," might also bring a strong initial reaction, but it builds respect without being rejecting. We couple these messages and boundaries with win-win choices to improve your relationship. The result is the initial stress that comes with change (the 10th floor kind, not the 100th floor kind), followed by adjustment and improvement in your relationship. This no-argument, no-avoidance, loving approach will give you power without creating a power struggle. Power struggles are created by arguing, when one person is having a verbal tug-of-war with the other. Getting on the same side ends the struggle. Reduced struggle means reduced (although not eliminated) risk of violence.

One further measure we take to reduce the risk of harm is to avoid negotiation.

Negotiating Can Lead to an Increased Risk of Violence

Negotiating is a good skill and is the proper solution to many differences that we have with others. But, if we resolve *most* of our differences with negotiations, we can become more and more resentful, until we feel like we have given too much in order to keep the peace with our partner. Overuse of negotiation in relationships creates resentment and distance and pressure slowly builds.

In negotiation, I give up something that I want in order to get or keep something else. You do the same. If we do that a lot, we end up giving up many things we want just to maintain what we have. So with each negotiation, something slips away a little. That slipping away is often our closeness, intimacy. The overuse of negotiation not only creates distance and resentment, it lessens respect and caring, and fuels our anger toward our partner. If this has happened in your relationship, your partner may compare his life with the way he would like it to be, see a large difference, and blame you for that difference. That's why rather than negotiating, we help our partner to get what he wants, and request the same from him. That creates a win-win. You and he will be able to look back and to see all that you have—thanks to each other.

That said, *occasional* negotiations are ok in a healthy relationship. But the best place for negotiation is with ourselves. We must give up some of our desires in order to have another that we value more. We must give up the satisfaction of arguing, or the comfort of avoiding, for example, in order to increase intimacy and oneness. The results of such self-negotiations will not lead to resentment because we will not blame our partners for them.

Why Stay in the Relationship If You Are in Danger?

I am not advising you to stay in a relationship if you are in danger. I am pointing out that danger is possible whether you are in a relationship or not; whether you are with this man or another man. Many people will advise you to leave a relationship with a man who threatens you or is violent towards you, and not give further advice or help. I think that advice is simplistic and even irresponsible—particularly if it comes from a professional. The reality is that leaving a relationship also presents risks (the very advice they give you could result in violence), and ignores the fact that many women will maintain their relationships even in the face of threats or violence.

Women who stay with a violent or potentially violent man, whether it is the right choice or not, need help not only to stay safe, but to earn respect, decrease the risk of future violence, improve communication, and develop trust. As long as there are ways to do that, women also need to have that information. Each person needs to be fully informed of what can be done as well as the risks involved. This is the standard in medicine and it needs to be the standard in mental health care and relationship improvement programs. Usually, there are multiple choices—each with risks and benefits.

Many of the women that I helped to have close relationships came to me at a time when their friends and family were telling them to divorce or breakup. While they may have done well had they divorced or broken up, I have never had a client regret improving her relationship.

Even if a woman wants to divorce, and perhaps especially if there is physical danger, she needs a way to communicate that to her husband, to present choices, to make it less of a shock, to help her husband to be rational and less reactive, and if possible, to provide the opportunity for reconciliation at a later time under the right conditions. Although divorce will always remain a tragedy, taking such preparations might do much to reduce the collateral damage that accompanies it.

"The hunger for love is much more difficult to remove than the hunger for bread." Mother Theresa

Section Two: The Interventions

"There are risks and costs to a program of action. But they are far less than the long-range risks and costs of comfortable inaction." John F Kennedy

8

LOVING (AND CHANGING) THE ANGRY MAN

Do you have an angry man? Regardless of how he was before, do you have an angry man now? This is usually not very hard to figure out. You can see it in his face. You can hear it in his voice. You can feel it in the way he talks to you and looks at you. This emotion, like other men's emotions is not without purpose. The purpose of anger is to change the behavior of others. Anger motivates him to force someone to do something (or not do something) if he can. If someone has enough anger and power, they will get compliance. And when others comply, the anger is switched off. It's no wonder then that angry men see other people as the reason for their anger. Because their anger is switched on and off according to what other people do. For angry men, that connection is clear. Do what an angry man wants and he is no longer angry until...he wants something else.

When he can't force compliance because of the risks involved or because of a lack of power, the anger is there anyway. It can be voiced or suppressed for hours and then burst out at innocent bystanders such as drivers on the highway, the dog, the kids, or you. On top of that, the really angry man can be provoked by anything—a slow checkout line, traffic congestion, someone disagreeing with him, someone not following through the way he wanted, or a bird pooping on his car.

The angry man believes that if only other people would change, then the world would be a nicer place and he wouldn't have to be angry. He feels like the victim. He's a sane man in an insane world. People make him wait, people are slow to act, and people don't do the right thing even when he carefully and persistently explains that it is the right thing to do. The angry man's anger makes perfect sense to him and he will not be talked out of it. His solution for fixing relationship problems is to fix you. To shape you into the way he thinks you should be. And to the extent that you are not that way, the problems are your fault (he thinks). Sound familiar?

The Challenges

The challenges in loving and helping the angry man are to protect yourself from his anger and to show him that his anger is hurting *him*. To show him that it is hurting you is not likely to be effective, since he would just say that you are causing the problem—that you are hurting yourself for not being the way he says you should be. Getting him to understand how you feel is not the route to go with an angry man.

If you clearly show him how his anger hurts himself, will he change? Not likely. It will only make his life seem really unfair to him. After all, he thinks his anger is caused by others so if his anger hurts him, it means other people are hurting him. He has to be the one to control his anger in order just to get along with people who don't deserve his kindness. This binds him and stresses him. Nobody likes to feel angry or stressed—even angry people.

The way he knows to feel better is to release his anger. But, if he does, then there is hell to pay for it. He will be in a "damned if I do, damned if I don't situation." It's no wonder that angry people are not happy people. Although he could learn to not become angry, that is very unlikely without outside help. And since he sees his anger as caused by others, he is very unlikely to seek help. He is much more likely to medicate his anger or to express it in "acceptable ways." What's an acceptable way? *Anything that other people accept.* If you are the person who accepts his anger, then who do you think will get the brunt of his anger? Other people will get Dr. Jekyll (Mr. Responsible), you will get Mr. Hyde (Mr. Mad Man).

The "hydraulic model" of anger has been given up by psychology. It used to be thought that anger builds up and by safely releasing it, people will be more calm. But, what was found in social psychology experiments is that people who are given a way to vent their anger (for example, by punching a punching bag) experience more and more anger.[8] Venting the anger becomes a reward for feeling angry. Hitting a punching bag to get out anger makes a person feel like punching and getting out anger more and more often. It feeds the problem. Anger needs to be starved, not fed. Anger needs to be deprived of satisfaction. Remove the opportunities to express anger and anger is expressed less and felt less. Angry kids should not play with violent toys. Angry husbands should not be allowed to vent on their wives.

To change the angry man, your goal will be to help him get what he wants from you but in a way that is not fueled by anger. You don't need to make him be "wrong" (a monumental bang-your-head-against-the-wall kind of task), you just need to help him be more effective in a better way. Given a choice between using a screwdriver or a hammer to install a screw, an angry man will choose a screwdriver. Why? Because it will work better, and *that* is what he really wants. He doesn't want to be angry. He only wants to change the world because he thinks he knows what's best for it. By showing him how to change *you* (without anger), you will be helping both of you to get exactly what you want. And, he will even be your ally in the process. You won't be taking his power away—you will be giving him another way to be powerful and more effective. And, you will help him to feel that way, while you enjoy his much improved

---

[8] Bandura, A. (1977), ***Social learning theory***, Prentice-Hall, Englewood Cliffs, N.J.

behavior. It is a win-win, which is the only way you can permanently improve a relationship.

The Components of Anger

Anger has both physical and psychological components. Physically, the sympathetic nervous system gets triggered. This is the system that readies the body for emergency response—whether to fight, flee, or freeze. Heart rate and respiration are increased by adrenaline. Because heart rate and blood pressure are increased, chronic anger can lead to stress-related illnesses such as clinical depression and cardiovascular disease, among others.[9]

Psychologically, higher reasoning processes are partially suppressed. In the midst of a fight is not the time to reason things out. Concentration and reasoning require calmness. In a rage, people can single mindedly do destructive things that they would never choose to do otherwise. It doesn't remove their responsibility for what they do, because they could have channeled their aggressiveness elsewhere. They could have walked out rather than shouting at the boss, punching a hole in the wall, or swearing at the kids. Regardless of who made him angry, the angry man is still responsible for how he responds.

Higher reasoning is not altogether gone. He's not likely to do something that risks his life, risks imprisonment, or damages something valuable. Never-the-less, an angry man may endanger himself by driving fast (risking his life and others), giving the finger to his boss (risking his job), or shouting at his wife (risking his relationship). Add drugs or alcohol into the mix and anything is possible. For this reason, if your husband has a drug or alcohol problem, that must be dealt with *before* trying to work on the anger.

Unless he is in a rage (an extreme and dangerous condition where reasoning is almost entirely gone), he will be able to think and talk,

---

[9] Cohen, S., Janicki-Deverts, D., and Miller, G.E. (2007). Psychological stress and disease. *The Journal of the American Medical Association, 298 (14)*, 1685-1687.

though in a more reactive fashion. The more calm he is, the more he will be able to reason. The less calm, the less he will be able to reason. The interventions that you will learn to do with him, while he is angry, don't require a lot of reasoning on his part. But, they do help to shift him toward desiring to reason, and therefore have a calming effect. A man who wants to reason can't also want to fight at the same time.

Differentiate Anger from Abuse

This chapter is about anger, it is not about abuse (see Chapter 7, Reducing the Risk of Violence). Although anger and abuse often occur together (especially with physical abuse), they also occur separately. This alone is enough to tell us two things: 1) abuse can occur without anger; and 2) anger can occur without abuse. Physical or emotional abuse has to do with *intent* to harm, whether or not harm actually results, and whether or not the person doing the abuse regrets his actions. So, if I accidentally trip you and you are injured, it is not abuse. But, if I intentionally trip you, meaning for you to be harmed, it is abuse whether you are harmed or not. Whether or not you are physically harmed should not be your line for differentiating abuse. Treat *any* attempt to harm you as abuse. You should have zero tolerance for abuse.

Although the physically abusive partner is dealt with elsewhere in this book, let me give you just a few guidelines for emotional abuse in case you run into these issues with your angry husband. These issues are common for my clients who have angry husbands.

First, angry people are often (though not always) loud. Being loud in itself is not abuse. Nobody likes getting yelled at, but someone shouting they love you is different from someone shouting they hate you. What is shouted makes the difference. Even whispered words can be abusive. It may hurt to hear "I hate you," whether it is shouted or whispered, but it is much better than a punch in the nose and is often the start of open communication. Many more couples hurt each other with silence than they do with words. Degrading comments about you, though, are abusive. "You are an *@#&&%!" is certainly abusive. Anything said to you that indicates you are some kind of objectionable object or worse than some objectionable thing, is abuse. "You are worse than a *@#&&%," for example, is abuse. Likewise, any threat to physically harm you is abuse—whether or not you are physically hurt. And if your husband raises his hand in a way indicating that he will strike you, he has already abused you.

The reason I make these distinctions is not for legal purposes. Legal definitions of abuse differ by culture and jurisdiction. I make the distinction here only so that you know when to deal with anger, and when to deal with abuse—the interventions are different. Any abuse that is happening must be dealt with first. The order of intervention for dealing with abusive husbands is: 1) keep yourself safe; 2) require an appropriate level of treatment; 3) require trust to be rebuilt; and 4) set specific consequences for what will happen if the abuse reoccurs. All of this is easier said than done, and as you read in Chapter 7 (Reducing the Risk of Violence), is best done with professional help.

Don't Expect His Cooperation—At First

When you help your angry man, you may be literally saving his life as well as his relationship with you. Unless he has been severely or repeatedly burned by his own anger, he is unlikely to agree with you that it's a problem. Helping him is going to involve teaching him that his anger both hurts him *and* is ineffective. The reason for that is that people will do what is harmful to themselves as long as they get something out of it. This is true for all damaging things that people do, including smoking, drinking, risky behavior, arguing, procrastinating, and many others. And because angry husbands see themselves as helping, he will make the sacrifice of hurting himself (with anger) if it helps you to change. With no payoff, it wouldn't be worth his upsetting himself. A smoker with no nicotine payoff would soon quit. We only pay the price when we get something for it. If you could make his anger totally ineffective with you, it would completely stop his anger toward you.

Stopping anger alone though, won't draw him any closer to you. For that, you will also need to help him be effective in getting what he wants from you. It is never bad for people to get what they want from you as long as it meets your needs too. In helping him not to be angry, you are not taking away his power or psychologically castrating him. Just the opposite—you are making him into your super man. And there is no reason he shouldn't feel that way. He can be your super man and you can be his super woman. "Superwoman" will be more exciting to him than "doormat woman." He will get more of what he wants without anger, because you will be more willing to help him. You will get more of what you want because he will want to help you and be less angry. Helping him will set up an upward spiral of increasingly better behavior from him, which gets an increasingly better response from you, which gets the both of you closer and closer. When I help my clients to create upward spirals, it reduces their need for future coaching. They can maintain their own progress.

How About His Anger with Other People?

Before you start expecting that his anger with the world is going to go away, remember that he has to have success with you before he can even think about behaving differently with others (including the kids). He can't do what he can't imagine and has never experienced. By helping him to have a new and more effective way of getting what he wants from you, you will have added an important relating tool to his tool chest. For a while, out of habit, he will first reach for his old tool, anger, with you, then check himself and pull out the new tool you will give him. Once he creates a new habit with you, he will still pull out his old tool of anger with other people. Why is that? Because he has had partial success that way. He has never used his new way with them. For now, you must not make his anger with others your problem. After you have dealt with his anger toward you, then you can deal with his anger toward the kids. Beyond that, he will have to decide how he is going to respond to others.

All or nothing thinking—that he must stop being angry with everybody—will not help you. Seeing his step of learning not to be angry with you as a step closer to better relationships with others (kids, coworkers, etc.) is a more realistic and helpful one.

Looking Closely at the Motivations Behind Your Husband's Anger

Why, *in particular*, is your husband so angry? In an earlier chapter, I talked about the general reasons for men's anger. Aside from these general reasons, it's helpful to look at the specific reasons why your husband is angry. The reason to do this, of course, is not to blame him or yourself, because blame won't do you any more good than it does your husband. He looks for blame. Make sure you don't fall into the same way of thinking. It would only make you more like him and that is not the way to go. When I say look at the reasons for your husband's anger, I mean make sense of it from *his* point of view. Everything that we do has some purpose or intention, even though the intentions may be misguided or not the right ones to help us accomplish what we are trying to achieve.

In the case of getting angry, we can connect it to four specific desires. These desires are either: 1) To get something done, 2) to get something right, 3) to get along, or 4) to get attention. These are the basic four motivations found by Brinkman and Kirschner.[10] Although we all have these four motivations to some extent, at times of stress we care about one of them much more than the others. Which one depends on our personality. When your husband is angry, he is very stressed. And at that time, he is concerned with one of these desires more than the others. It will help to know which one your husband is typically concerned about when he is angry.

For example, let's suppose that your husband is trying to fix the car. But, instead of fixing it, he is getting increasingly upset. We can guess that in this situation, he is probably motivated both to "get it

---

[10] Brinkman, R. and Kirschner, R. (2003). *Dealing with difficult people: 24 Lessons for bringing out the best in anyone.* New York: McGraw-Hill.

right" (get the car to work right) and "get it done" (so he can move on to something else). Unless you have some way to help him get it right and get it done, you had best stay out of his way. Interrupting him at this time may be a nuisance to him—an interruption of his goals to get it right and get it done. If he sees you as an obstacle to getting it done, then he will target his anger at you. If he *does* get angry at you, then you can direct a question directly at his motives. For example, if you ask, "How can I help you to get this done?" or "What do you need to get it working?" he is likely to tell you. Other questions which emphasize the difficulty he is having, such as "What's wrong with it?" or "Why can't you get it working?" are something like pouring gas on a fire because it intensifies the frustration he feels. You may be trying to help him to be more relaxed, or to be emotionally supportive, but he will probably think of the talking as just taking time away from what he's trying to do. So, leave him alone to do it. Bringing him a drink (coffee, juice) without staying to talk would be a nicely supportive action.

Another motivator for your husband's anger may be his desire "to get along." If he is trying to get along with you, the kids, or someone else, but it doesn't go so well, he may become very angry. Especially if he talks about how things are "not fair" because he does so much for others and he just gets grief in return. People with poor social skills often have this kind of anger. Because they are ineffective at getting others to respond to them in a positive way, despite their best efforts, they find something wrong with the other person. It really is a kind of self protection. Either other people are messed up or they are. The angry person defensively and automatically believes it is others.

You know that if he could treat other people better, they would treat him better, and then he would be happier. Because he wants to get along. If other people are nice to his face, they may dislike him behind his back. The benefit is that they get along better with him, but they don't have a better *relationship* with him. It's an approach that won't work for you. Just treating him better, kinder, nicer, or being more patient, *will* result in his being less angry. But, his social skills will not have changed and he will be no more sensitive to your needs than before. It won't be long before you think again, "Why do I bother?" Placate your mother-in-law, not your husband.

To make a permanent improvement in your relationship, you will need to do something different than just trying to get along with him. You will need to do something that *demonstrates* to him that his anger hurts him. That it hurts you is not going to make that much difference to him because he doesn't feel responsible for your "foolish" actions.

Your husband is no psychopath—he does care about you. He cares whether you feel hurt or not, but he does not feel *responsible* for your hurt. Because, in his way of thinking, you could behave in a different way and get a better result. The more he cares about you, the more angry he may get with you for not behaving in a "better" way. If you can follow that line of reasoning, then you can understand how your husband can love you so much and be so angry with you at the same time. (If he didn't care about you, he wouldn't bother to spend any effort on helping you to change).

Once your husband really learns how to get along (if that is his primary motivation), you can have a much closer relationship than before. You will also have a much happier man. So, do be aware if your husband is trying to "get things done," trying to "get things right," or to "get along." On the surface they look the same, but the motivations are different. He is either angry because he can't get things done, can't get things right, or can't get along. There is also one other possibility.

One final motivation for anger is the desire to "get attention." Some people only get attention by being angry. Others get angry because they don't get attention for other things. Whether it comes from their family background or genetics, the result is the same—some people need more attention than others. We all have a need for attention, but some men, when under stress, need more attention than others. Their anger will both be at the injustice of not receiving attention, and a way to force attention (even if it is negative attention). Any attention at all is better than no attention for people who need it. A very hungry person will eat from a dumpster; a person who strongly needs attention will take it from anyone. And, if no one will give it, it will be created. If you can recognize this need in your husband, you can see it as his desire to connect with, and get approval from you. These are very appropriate qualities in a husband—when he goes about getting them in a good way.

Unfortunately, he is mainly getting your attention in an angry way or is attempting to teach you to give him more attention (angry people are angry because of the imagined failings of others; therefore angry partners try to teach you or fix you). At an unconscious level, the thought is something like this—"If I do things worthy of attention, and you don't pay attention to me, then something must be wrong with you." These men may also be the easiest for others to seduce since they are motivated to get attention. A dog who is underfed at home may raid the neighbor's garbage. I have had many women tell me that they were surprised that the woman their husband was having an affair with was much less attractive than they are. But, the answer is simple—their husbands were getting something they needed from the other woman. He may have needed her to look at him more than he needed to look at her!

Does this mean that if a man is angry because he is not getting the attention he wants, that it's his wife's fault? Not at all. A wife is never to blame for her husband's behavior or how he acts on his feelings. His anger may in fact be driving you away and taking away your desire to pay attention to him. You may also feel that any attention you give him just rewards him for his angry behavior. And that would be partly true. If you only give him attention when he is angry, then you will be reinforcing his angry behavior. Do give him attention for positive things, even if small and ordinary. Do make sure you deal with him effectively when he is angry. Then his attention seeking methods will shift in a positive direction. The following two things always occur together in an effective intervention—1) stopping the bad behavior (or preventing its success), and, 2) introducing a good behavior that creates his *desired* success. (What he really desires will support his relationship with you, since your relationship is important to him).

Regardless of whether your husband's behavior is motivated by the need to get something right, to get something done, to get along, or to get attention, you are not going to be able to change these motivations. Nor should you want to. They are actually very good motivations. What you will be helping your husband to do is to get these needs satisfied. You will do that in a way that promotes your relationship with him. And you will make his current angry methods for satisfying these motivations *totally* ineffective. That word *totally* is key since people will continue to do whatever is partially successful.

When He Changes from Something, He Has To Change To Something

Some women demand their husband change but don't provide a means for him to have success. Since angry men see their anger as caused by others, changing on their own is very difficult. If he has no way to be successful with you, then he will either end the relationship with you, or emotionally withdraw from you. He could also shift from anger into depression. But if you help him, his behavior with you will dramatically improve. Everybody wants to have success and to feel successful. That goes for you and it goes for your husband. He does not want to be rejected.

There are many good ways to get things done, to get things right, to get along, and to get attention. He needs to learn them and use them. When you help him to be good at those ways with you, you make him a more powerful man, a more attractive man, and a man you will want to be with more often. There is no trickery involved or deception involved in the interventions that teach him. There is also no fighting or coercion. This all happens simply by changing the way you interact with him. Next, we will get into the specifics of making goals for relationship improvement.

Making a Plan

You have a husband who is often angry and it's a result of his habits, beliefs, and motivations. What should be your goal in this situation? To change his beliefs? To changes his motivations? To change his emotions? No. As always, the goal should be to improve your relationship. Although it's tempting to make your goal to stop his anger, it's an unrealistic one that will cause more problems (as you've probably already found out). Why? Because everyone gets angry. The only difference among people is what makes us angry and how we express our anger. When wives make their goal to stop their husband's anger, they soon come to the conclusion that the only way to stop their husband's anger is to avoid doing things that make their husband angry. But, because their husbands get angry so easily, what really results is less and less communication with their husbands. This, in turn, results in more and more emotional distance. A downward spiral. A goal of stopping anger results in a more distant relationship. That is why your goal should not be to stop, or prevent, his anger. If that is what you have been doing, *your* actions must stop if you are to get closer. The goal is a better relationship, not an emotional lobotomy for your husband.

As a relationship coach, I talk with people every day who are so focused on fixing their problems with their partners that they've forgotten why they are with them in the first place. "I just want the fights to stop," "I want him to pay attention to me and listen to me," and the saddest one—"I just want to know how to get him back (when he has left)." In all of these cases, I do help people to get what they want, but we start with the understanding that fixing the problem is only one step toward a bigger goal—the goal to get closer. If you don't get closer, what good are these other things? And if you make fixing the problem your goal, then there is the danger that you will do what is bad for the relationship in order to fix the problem. For example, if you see your husband's shouting as "the problem," it could result in your avoiding him, avoiding talking about sensitive topics, or even threatening to leave him to make him stop. While these things will fix this shouting problem (temporarily), they result in other problems. Focusing on problems alone cannot take you where you want to go.

If you make getting closer to your husband your goal, then it will be necessary to work on his shouting, but you will be able to clearly see that avoiding talking or making threats won't help because they won't make you closer. Every intervention we do must work toward that long term goal of closeness if you and your husband are to be happy with and maintain the changes. My clients and I spend our first few sessions together making a long term plan for getting closer. Then we can easily identify steps to end the problem and move the relationship forward. Working on the problem becomes the same as working on a better future, and that's very motivating for both husband and wife.

You can also make some long term plans on your own as your first step. One way to do that is to imagine that you have fixed the immediate problem. Your husband no longer shouts at you, blames you, tries to change you, etc. Don't worry right now about how you will do that. If your husband has made this change, then what? What would be your next step? Would it automatically make you closer, or would you still need to learn to talk to each other, to work together, and to keep growing? In other words, changing his problem behavior is not all that is needed to become close.

Example of Making a Plan to Reach Goals

Start with your long term goal.

Long Term Goal: Improve our relationship

Then write out each of the elements that you need to reach that goal. For this example, let's say it's stopping anger, communicating well, doing things together, and working together on the future. List each one of these elements as a separate step, in the order that makes most sense.

Step One: *Stop fighting;*
Step Two: *Do more things together;*
Step Three: *Talk more about our thoughts and feelings;*
Step Four: *Make plans together for the future.*

At this point, you don't need to figure out how these steps will be accomplished, but just need to put them in an order that makes sense. It's obviously hard to do things together if there is a lot of fighting, so stopping the fighting has to come first. And you're going to need to be able to share thoughts and feelings before you can start planning your future together. When you have such a plan laid out, you can break each step into two or more smaller steps:

Step One: *(Stop fighting)*
            Work on my own anger.
            Use an anger intervention with my husband (as in this book).

Step Two: *(Do more things together)*
            At first, find out more of my husband's interests.
            Do some short activities near home.
            As things get better, do longer activities further from home.

Step Three: *(Talk more about our thoughts and feelings).*
            At first, talk more about general, non-sensitive topics.
            Then, about things we disagree about but are not so sensitive about.
            Then about sensitive things, but with support and understanding for each other.

Step Four: *(Make plans for the future)*
            At first, make only short range plans for the future.
            Then, make longer range plans.

In this example, a four step plan has become a 10 step plan. Each of the previous steps has been broken down into smaller, more manageable steps. Each of these steps can also be broken down into more steps. Making more steps does not make accomplishing the goal longer or harder—it makes it *faster and easier.* You can easily climb a flight of many steps to the second floor, but if your staircase only had four steps, it would be very hard to go to the second floor. It would take a lot more time and effort. This example plan is just that—an example. Everybody's plan is different. Yours will be, too. I highly recommend you make one before you start working on dealing with your husband's anger. Although making a plan takes time initially, it greatly shortens the overall process. Plans separate out successful people from people who try hard, but have only short term success. You want to make sure that your success is long term. First write the big steps, then break them into smaller steps. Continue that process until the size of the steps feels manageable to you.

With your plan in place, you can now see that learning to deal with your husband's anger is an early step on the way to many good things that will require many small but doable steps. Relationships are always works in progress. But that process can be an enjoyable and creative one.

Your Plan is for You *and* Your Husband

Another reason to have a goal of relationship improvement (rather than just fixing the problem) is to motivate your husband. If you make your goal to stop his anger, he will rightly perceive that you are trying to fix him and just for the purpose of fixing him. If someone is trying to fix you, what does that mean? It means that they don't accept you the way you are. That you are defective. That you are not good enough. Most husbands (and wives, too) would rebel against their spouse's attempts to fix them. And, if he is a lot more stubborn than you, and has more energy than you, it is only a matter of time before he gets you to give up. He won't be your ally in change if your end goal is to fix him.

When your goal is to make the relationship better, *for both of you*, then he has something to gain by the changes you want. Even more than that, he has something to lose by not changing. In my job as a coach, most people tell me that their partner does not want to work on the relationship. What we find, though, is that their partner does not want to work on being fixed. When they can see what's in it for them and what they would miss out on by not working on it, they become motivated. Spouses are eager to participate when they: 1) are not the focus of the problem, and 2) see what is in it for them.

Although you might think that just being less angry would be a motivator for your husband, you must remember that he sees his anger as being caused by other people, *and* he's used to it. Giving up anger to him is equivalent to giving up altogether, or giving in. And, goals of being able to talk more together do not motivate most men, who see talking as a tiresome job. Get him to see beyond that—to what good things can come to him that he wants, and he will hesitantly get on board. Unfortunately, though, he won't be ready to listen and take you seriously until *after* you effectively do the first steps of dealing with his anger. It is imperative that you succeed in doing that.

Getting Ready for the Next Step

Hopefully, I've convinced you to make improving the relationship for both you and your husband your goal. This will help you to see your husband's anger as an obstacle to both of you and not as some ignorant way that your husband likes to be. No one likes to be angry. Just by your having this perspective, your husband will be more cooperative. The things you will say to him when you are dealing with his anger will be focused on making the relationship better for both of you. They will sound more caring and less blaming. Blame won't motivate your husband any more than it motivates you. Dealing with his anger is something you are doing for him, as well as you. It's an expression of love. It's an "I'm so damn tough because I love you so damn much" approach that is both respectable and acceptable to men. Next, you will learn the intervention part of dealing with anger (step one in the example plan).

Making Changes

If you have skipped to this section, please go back and read the first part of this chapter. Just as in painting your house, the prep work is important for a good final product. If something's worth doing, it's worth doing right.

Stopping Ineffective Behaviors

If you want to fill a glass with orange juice, but it's already full of water, what do you need to do first? You first need to empty out the water. If you just tried to add juice without emptying out the water, the glass would overflow and the juice would be watered down and weak. So it is with changing your interactions with your husband. You can't start doing new things until you figure out what you are doing wrong, and stop it. Otherwise, you will try to improve at the same time you are contributing to the problem. The result? Ineffective, watered down, and inconsistent results.

To take another example, imagine that you were trying to lose weight by eating more fruit and vegetables. Sounds good, but if you continued to fill up on potato chips and cake, it wouldn't matter how much broccoli you ate. The junk food would maintain your weight. Clearly, you would need to give up the junk food, then eat healthy foods. In the case of chocolate cake, puddings, and potato chips, it's obvious. But what about in regard to your angry husband? What junk is maintaining the problem? Let's start to figure that out.

First, think about the last time he got angry. What was it about? What did you do? Did you get angry too? Did you get loud? Or become quiet? Did you defend yourself? Do something else? How did what you did help or not help? Are there things you usually do to prevent his anger? Even if they work, are they helping your relationship? Take the time to write down what you usually do. Go ahead, get a pen or pencil and write it down. To be *really* good at this, write down both what happens in the short term and what will happen in the long term if you keep doing it. For example, if you fight back, does it stop his angry behavior (a short term gain)? Will it lead to things gradually getting better (a long term gain) or worse (a long term loss) as your relationship goes on? Has it resulted in his getting more and more comfortable in showing his anger (another long term loss)? Does it make you feel closer or more distant? Try to find the *pattern* (what he does and what you do). There is always a pattern.

If you wrote out the answers to these questions, you should have a pretty good idea of what doesn't work and what actually makes the problem worse. These are the behaviors that you are going to need to replace. It won't be easy for you, because the things you do are partially working for you, even if they are hurting your relationship. When you replace these behaviors with more effective ones, however, your relationship will improve. Looking at the long term plan you created earlier will help you to give up the partially successful behaviors for new ones.

Don't think for a minute that I just want you to be patient with your husband. There is no way that I want you to be patient in the face of your husband's anger. Giving up what you do now does not mean becoming patient. Your husband's anger is like a fire, burning your relationship down. It is not a time for patience. You will have to take action—it's not just going to stop all by itself. Let's make sure your actions really put the fire out and keep it out.

Starting Effective Behaviors

As we saw earlier, there are different causes of anger and there are different presentations of anger. You need to match your husband's motivation to your intervention. What works for one relationship may only cause more problems for another. For present purposes, I will tell you how to deal with the man who gets angry and withdraws, as well as the man who has angry outbursts.

Dealing with the Angry Withdrawn Husband

This is the kind of husband who gets upset and then goes somewhere on his own to deal with his anger or to punish you with brooding, sulking, and silence. Just like all angry behaviors, they are intended to force something from you. This is the easiest behavior to deal with. Simply let him go pout, sulk, cool off, or whatever he is doing. Though he is angry, his anger is actually not the main problem. It is poorly communicating about problems and blaming rather than problem solving. It is a communication and collaboration issue and not an anger issue. If you are ok with letting him go cool off, his separation at this time will not be a punishment for you. You also won't seem so needy if you are ok with letting him go. Making a mad dash to stop him only encourages this kind of behavior. Look at his behavior as a kind of self control (which it is). Be glad he pouts rather than shouts. After he has come out of "withdrawal," you can use the five step anger follow-up that I present later in this chapter.

Anger and Abusive Language

Loudness is one thing, abusive language is another. Abusive words should not be tolerated *at all*. Treat verbal abuse as though he hit you or threatened to. Leave immediately, unless it is dangerous to do so. Get professional help as soon as possible. No matter whether it happens the first time or has gone on for years, you must take this very seriously. Under-reacting is the biggest mistake you can make with any abuse, of any kind. If you believe that verbal abuse is acceptable to give or receive, then you need help as much as the woman who believes it is acceptable to hit or be hit.

Dealing With Angry Outbursts: Step One

Loudness can be irritating, but there is nothing wrong about loudness itself. Rock music is loud, thunder is loud, and roller coasters are loud. Unless he is shouting in your ear, it is not abuse for him to yell. Public loudness, though, should not be tolerated. If he is loud in public, then vote with your feet. Leave the scene from the moment he gets loud. If you need to call a taxi to get home, do it. Taking immediate action each and every time will quickly build respect and quickly end the behavior. If he tries to physically restrain you, deal with the issue as abuse, rather than anger. When I help women to make these changes, their husbands typically change within a week or two—even if the behavior has gone on for years. It is well worth whatever the taxi costs.

In private, remember that you can't help someone stop presenting themselves to you in a hostile way by being hostile yourself. So, if he is loud, you need to speak softly, but naturally, and matter of factly. If he is on a roll with his anger, break up the rhythm of it by getting a cup of coffee, feeding the dog, etc. Remember to be nice as you do so. Offer to make him a cup, etc. What you are striving for here are two things: 1) to get him to stop of his own accord (learn self-control); and 2) to not let him get rewarded by your getting upset. Another way to break up his angry tirade is to take him into another setting. For some men, their tirade stops once they are in the public eye. So, talking it out at a restaurant, coffee shop, or on a walk in the park may break up the tirade. Other men don't care, though. Whether he stops or not, listen carefully to what he is saying and don't tell him to stop. Telling him to stop would put him in a position to defy you and create a larger conflict. The next step will teach you something better to do instead.

Dealing With Angry Outbursts: Step Two

When your husband is full of anger, and is emptying it out on you, break up the rhythm as stated above, but don't interrupt with information, corrections, or defensiveness. Let him go on, even if he says you have six eyes and stones are good to eat. Interrupting with comments or corrections will just turn up the intensity and that is not an effective thing to do—no matter how wrong he may be in what he is saying. At some point, he will start to repeat what he is saying. He will do this to make sure that you "get it." If you are used to interrupting or fighting with him, then the way he usually knows that you "get it" is by hearing what you have to say. But, now, you are not saying anything. If you didn't say anything and let him continue to repeat himself he would escalate his anger to ensure a reaction from you. That would not be helpful. So, the time for you to interrupt comes when he *starts to repeat* what he is saying.

From his first repetition, stop him (it is ok at this point) and restate to him his main points. Just say, "Let me see if I got this right." Then restate his points without adding corrections or comments. Also, affirm that he has a right to be angry (everyone has a right to their feelings). Be careful *not* to add anything of your own. This is not the time for talking things out or dealing with issues. You will have your chance to talk things out with him after you learn to manage his anger. You can't do both at the same time. When you restate his points to him, if you leave something out, most likely that will come shooting back at you. So, try again to restate his points. "Ok, let me try that again…." But, don't argue, don't defend. No matter how wrong he is. Restating his points does not mean that you are admitting to accusations or that he is right. They are just assurance that you heard him. He must not be rewarded for his angry behavior and if you remain calm, it will come off making him look bad. The first few times you do this will unsettle him, because he doesn't know this routine. He's used to the old one.

This is the start of teaching him it is ok to be angry, but that communication with you is going to happen differently. Telling him so won't help. Giving him this book won't help. Only by making these changes will he be able to get the message. You're not hurting him, you are teaching him to communicate in a better way. Step-by-step. As you are doing it, you are also learning it. After you learn it, then he will catch on and learn it too. First you learn and then you do, then he learns and then he does. In that order, always. It takes him two steps to catch up to you, so be patient.

If, he calms down really well, and you are calm too, then talking right away is fine. If you can't or he can't (and don't try to "make" him), then just keep using this process of listening and restating his points until he runs out of things to say. If he starts to say the same thing as before and you have already restated these things well, then tell him you already heard that. "I heard that part already. What part am I missing?" He will then either make some kind of declaration and storm out (in that case, let him; see the example on page 3), or he will ask for some response from you. With the following information, you will be prepared for either of these reactions.

If he asks for some response, make an *appointment* with him to talk about it at a time you are both calm and at least one hour later. If he refuses, that is ok. He will either forget the issue, or will become angry about it again at another time. When he does, go through the process again of listening and restating. If he again demands answers, then make an appointment to talk about it when you are both calm. Don't give in to pressure to talk right away or change won't happen.

This is really not as difficult a process as it sounds, though it will frustrate him. It will ensure that his angry communication style no longer works with you. You will have pulled the plug. But, you will be opening the door to him talking in a better way and getting the answers he wants. Remember, the old way must stop if new ways are to begin. And you must be the one to stop them, because he is not going to stop on his own.

Write down the time for your meeting, and keep your meeting. Don't let him pull you into talking about it before the meeting time. "We've set time aside to talk about that, and I'm going to wait until then." At the meeting, use good communication skills. If he gets out of control, go back to the process for managing his angry episodes (completely listening and then restating his main points). Set a different time to continue talking. Sticking with a simple anger response routine will change everything without your needing to fight about anything. Isn't that worth the stress that it takes to learn it? Two weeks of intervention compared with years of anger is a sweet deal.

Example of Dealing With Angry Outbursts

Your husband Jim becomes angry when you come home an hour late. Rather than defend yourself at that time, you deal with his anger by listening to him carry on until he starts to repeat himself. You then stop him, and restate the things that he has said to you.

Jim: "Why can't you come home on time?! You know I have to A and B and it's your job to 1, 2, 3, and 4 (kind of a speech about never coming home on time or caring about anybody but yourself, etc.).

You: (In the middle of his presentation) "Oh, Jim, I'm going to have a cup of coffee, would you like one?) (You make coffee, he follows, continuing).

Jim: "I don't want any coffee! All you care about is what you want. Tonight, you didn't come home on time . . ."

You: (Recognizing that Jim is starting to repeat himself, you stop him by putting up your hand, like a stop signal). "Ok, I heard this part, so let me see if I got this right. Your angry, and you have a right to be. Your angry because I came home late. You have an A and B, and it's my job to 1, 2, and 3, and I don't care about anybody but myself. Is that right?"

Jim: "You always do this kind of thing to me."

You: "Oops, I left that out. Your angry because I came home late. You have an A and B, it's my job to 1, 2, 3; I don't care about anybody but myself, and I always do that to you. Is that right?"

Jim: "Are you trying to be sarcastic?"

You: "No. I'm just making sure that I got your points correct."

Jim: "Well, what are you going to do about it?"

You: "Jim, if you would like to talk about this and work on this together, then we can schedule a time when we are both calm and can focus on this."

Jim: "I just want you to tell me right now. I don't need to have any stupid discussion."

You: "It's either at a time we agree to, or not at all. I'm not going to argue with you."

Jim: "I'm not arguing, I just want to know what you are going to do about it."

You: (You walk away. You are ready to leave the house if necessary. You refuse to argue or discuss. You end up leaving the house for an hour. When you return, Jim is silent and sulking. You just let him be. You write in your journal how you did a very hard thing today for the sake of your marriage. You continue your relationship with Jim just as if nothing had happened).

After you come back, it's important not to be rejecting, though if he is still sulking, let him. When he stops sulking, be positive again. It's important for your husband to get the message that he's not being rejected. You're just changing the way the two of you communicate when he is angry. Also, don't try to explain it to him unless he asks.

The first time is the toughest. But, as I said before, the more frequently your husband is angry, the quicker you will be able to change the way the two of you communicate. In my experience, in severe cases, women will end up needing to leave their home for an hour several times the first week. Does it sound like a hassle? Just consider, several hours of finding something to do to change a pattern that has gone on for many years—with no fighting! At first, he will just try to get you to go back to your old way. He won't want to schedule. But then, he will surprise you by scheduling a talking time with you. That's when you move on to the next step—talking.

The Scheduled Talk, A New Beginning

At this point your husband has either calmed down considerably on his own after his initial anger, or you have scheduled a time to talk about what is bothering him. After scheduling with you, he may change his mind. If he does, you don't need to worry about it. He eventually will follow through. Change is a step-by-step process. If he scheduled, but didn't follow through, he made one more step than before. For now, I am going to assume that he wants to talk and is prepared to talk. Maybe for one of the first times in the marriage, you have the ball. Here are the five steps you will follow. You don't need to memorize them, but it's good to review them beforehand.

It's ok to have the steps written on a note card to remind you and to help you stay on track. There is nothing secret about what you are doing. If your husband wants to see the card, that is fine.

The Five Step Anger Follow-Up

This will be as unnatural to him as wearing high heel shoes. You will need to lead here, just as you did when he was angry. You won't always have to lead, of course—just until he can lead the two of you in a good direction. You had been letting his anger lead the both of you into the ditch. Now, you are making important changes that won't feel natural to either of you. It is a temporary transition. Coaches, like myself, help you to do things that feel unnatural so you can get what you want. Here are the <u>five basic steps for your meeting</u>:

Step 1. Wait for him to ask "So what are we supposed to do now?" or some such. Don't just jump in. This allows him to initiate the process. When he makes his remark (a false lead), tell him he was getting really angry with you before, so you know this talk is important to him.

Step 2. Tell him that as long as you both can stay calm, you want to know what is making him really angry.

Step 3. If he says he already told you, or you already know, tell him that you just wanted to be sure there wasn't more, but you are glad that he shared that with you (remember, you don't want to move him away from sharing things with you, just away from having to be really angry in order to share).

Step 4. Tell him that now, you want to know what he wants you *to do* and how that would be good for the relationship.

Step 5. Thank him for working on having a close relationship with you because that is what you really want. If possible, give him a hug.

Example Five Step Anger Follow-Up

(Continuing with the example of Jim, above).

Jim: "Ok, I'm here. Now what?"

You: "I know you had something really important to talk to me about. As long as we can stay calm, we can talk about it now. If things get out of hand, then I will stop right away."

Jim: "Whatever."

You: "So, Jim, I really want to hear what you have to say and to know how I can help."

Jim: "You already know what I want."

You: "I think so, but I wanted to make sure there isn't something I missed."

Jim: "You always come home late without calling and I don't like it. You don't care about my time or my needs."

You: "What would you like me to do that would be good for our relationship?"

Jim: "Come home on time or call when you are going to be late."

You: "Ok. I will."

Jim: "Well, that was easy."

You : "I liked it. Can I get a hug?"

Now it's time for your author to read your mind. You are thinking that if it was really that easy to talk with your husband, you wouldn't need this book. Of course, I know that, but I wanted to show you what you are shooting for. Now, I will show you how to handle a couple of problems that are likely to occur.

Problem #1 Anger Flaring Up Again During Your Talk

...Jim: "You know damn well what I want. Don't expect me to ....!"

You: (Because Jim has lost his temper, go back to your anger management technique: 1) listen and distract; 2) restate his main points; 3) reschedule; and 4) leave, if necessary.

This is going to happen a few times. Expect it rather than be upset by it.

It's natural for your husband's anger to flare up the first couple of times you try this. Don't see it as sign of failure. It's part of the natural change process. Your following through by ending the conversation will get you a little more respect. You can only get respect if you do what you say. Continue to show your husband that his anger no longer works with you. As I said before, the more hostile the husband, the faster this will work. In this process you don't actually need to worry about his behavior at all. You only need to focus on what you are supposed to do. You know what to do if he is cooperative. You know what to do if he is not. Either way, it is ok. You *are* making progress. Change doesn't happen in one step.

Problem #2 You Lose *Your* Temper

...Jim: "I wish you weren't so selfish..."

You: "Selfish! I work my ass off...!...Wait...I blew it. We will have to try again later."

See, you get to be human, too. No one said you needed to do this perfectly for things to work out. Just keep working at it until you can do it right and do it consistently. Also, your catching yourself like this is a good example of self control for your husband. Imagine how proud you would be of your kids or sister or friend if they handled things this way.

Problem #3 The Laundry Gets Dumped on Your Head

...Jim: "Where do I start. Let's see. You don't come home on time. You don't like sex. You spend more time with your mother than you do with me..."

You: "Jim. We set this time aside to talk about what was upsetting you last night. Either we can focus on that or we can end this conversation. Which do you prefer?"

Angry people often pull out a laundry list of items to attack you with. By following this "one topic" rule for discussions, you stop that process. I suggest you *always* follow this practice, whether it is with your husband, your kids, or anyone else. Otherwise, you will get sucked into a fight.

These three problems will show you how to handle many situations. Anything more severe (abusive language or behavior), gets dealt with first, before working on anger. (I know I say this many times, but I don't want you to get abused).

You will notice in the example above, that you ask your husband what he would like you to do that is "good for the relationship." This is a little unnatural perhaps, but you want him to learn to think relationally rather than just about what he wants or you want. It will give you a good basis for disagreeing when he wants something that would be bad for the relationship.

Example of Shifting His Focus to the Relationship

You: "Jim, what would you like me to do, that would be good for our relationship?"

Jim: "I want you to come home every night, on time."

You: "If I did that, I would feel like you were controlling me. I don't think that would help our relationship. And I don't want to become distant from you."

By ending your response with how it would be bad for your husband, you involve him in the process. Angry men are most concerned about how things will affect them. Even when you disagree, show how you are thinking about him (which you are honestly doing if you are doing what is best for the relationship). Also, angry as he is, he doesn't want to be rejected. He wants you to need him as much as he needs you. Most angry men have a lot in common with scared little boys.

Handling Hostile Questioning

As long as you are following the five step procedure for dealing with anger outbursts, some hostility in his questions during step two is acceptable. Actually, he has made a big step just to follow through with a controlled talk. It is one step in the right direction. He will change best, if like you, he is allowed to change one step at a time. It's also a lot easier to do the intervention if you only need to work on one step at a time. I don't mean that you tolerate abuse or let him get out of hand. Those things you will deal with, of course. What I mean is that if he is not talking in a nice way or has a mean face or sharp voice and asks you questions, try to let it slide. If you can, try to ignore that face or voice, and just focus on the talk That is what he is learning to do. He won't always look or sound hostile—just in this early transition phase. The better he gets at communicating, the less hostile he will be. So hang in there!

If he says he wants to know why you were late (the above example), then just tell him (without defending yourself). There is never a need to defend yourself from a question. For example, "I was late because a friend of mine just lost her husband and needed someone to talk to. So we had a coffee and talked." (Don't expect Jim to agree with your reason whatever it is).

Example of Handling Hostile Questioning

Jim: "Why were you late anyway? You know you are supposed to be here at 6:00."

132

You: *"I was late because a friend of mine just lost her husband and needed someone to talk to. So we had a coffee and talked."*

Jim: *"Oh. Well, you could have called."*

You: *"I wish that I did. You have a good point."*

Jim: *"You should care more about me than about your friend."*

You: *"Of course I love you more. But, if I can't help my friends, then I will start to resent you and pull away from you. It wouldn't be good for you."*

Your mindreading author is thinking again that that last line is a little hard for you to swallow. It would be so much easier for you to say, "It wouldn't be good for us." And that is exactly the thing to say when you are working together calmly as a couple. In other words, it's coming up for you in the future. But, right now, you are dealing with an angry man who is in a new and stressful situation. He needs extra support as you help him to change. None of these things you are doing now are permanent. They are just transition moves.

As you can see, there is never any arguing or apologizing in these methods, though there is concern and a strong message of love. Your aim is to be tough and loving at the same time. It's what everyone wants and few people get. Your husband will soon learn that being angry with you results in "The Scheduled Talk." And, he will start to say "forget it" most of the time rather than schedule a talk. It's very important that at that time, you do forget it. His "forget it" is an off switch he is using to get more self control. Don't see it as an on switch for your own arguing. Besides learning to stop himself with "forget it," he will also learn more and more that he can talk and tell you what he wants without you attacking him. That sets the stage for sharing down the road (part of your long-term plan, right?).

Helping Your Husband with His Anger Will Lead To Better Things

I think you can start to see how this intervention for anger is actually part of a larger plan for restoring intimacy and promoting trust, respect, and sharing in your relationship. It's the same intervention that I help many of my clients with on their way to their ultimate goal of a close relationship. After this intervention there are many more good things you can go on to do with your husband that would not have been possible before. Each step you take in working on your relationship is like climbing 300 feet up a mountain—it allows you to see more and more of the view.

Summary of Intervention Skills

So far, you have read about a number of things you can do. You also have some tools to help you deal with things that your husband may do. I have intentionally given you advice for handling the toughest of situations. Not because you are likely to need all of them, but because you have them, you don't need to worry about what to do if they happen. On the next page is a checklist of reminders for you. Follow them all to maximize your success.

You Will Soon Become the Special Irreplaceable Woman in His Life

You will probably not be the first woman in his life to confront him about his anger, but you may be the first woman to really help him with it. Because you will probably be the only woman who knew how. If you follow the steps of this intervention consistently, he will get to the point where he skips the angry outburst and says that you two need to set a time to talk. When this happens, make sure you make it a priority to do so. If the way you taught him stops working, then he will return to his old way. If you teach him to talk, but then don't make yourself available, the only other thing he knows how to do is lose his temper. Give him plenty of love and affection for his positive changes. The woman who waits for her husband to completely change before she gives affection, waits too long. So, yes, that means that you need to be willing to give love and affection *long before you feel like it*.

134

Intervention Skills Reminders

☐ Abusive behavior—get professional help; treat before anger problems; never overlook abuse!

☐ Addictions—treat before anger, but after abuse.

☐ Angry outbursts—use the two step intervention for stopping the outburst.

☐ If you can't stop an angry outburst with the two step intervention, then leave for 10 minutes to one hour.

☐ Help him to have success with you—it's where your true power is.

☐ His questions—answer them during the five step anger follow –up without defending yourself or apologizing.

☐ Hug—great way to end the five step anger follow-up; make it at least a 30 second hug; quickie hugs are for aunts.

☐ Husband says "forget it" when you try to schedule a talk—just forget it; it was his concern anyhow.

☐ Husband wants to know what you are doing—tell him you are learning to save your relationship with him because you love him.

☐ Making mistakes—everyone does, just get back on track.

☐ Prevent him from having success with you with his harmful anger.

☐ Outburst in public—leave by yourself.

☐ Recurrence of hot temper during the five step anger follow-up—go back to the two step intervention for handling angry outbursts.

☐ Stick to one subject or schedule another talk for another topic.

☐ Work only on changing his angry behavior until it is much better. Working on more things right now will overwhelm the both of you and lead to failure.

The Calm between the Storms

It doesn't always rain, even in Seattle, and your husband is not always angry. There is important work for you to do with your husband during these times of relative calm. It's important to realize that the changes you are making when he is angry are going to shake him up. Not only has he never had such an experience with a woman, he doesn't know what is going on in your mind and what is going to happen next. Angry men are often very insecure men. He may think that your refusal to either fight or back down means that you are getting ready to leave him, or that you have found another man. Although you know that's not what it means, he doesn't know that. Although it might make you feel powerful and like the tables are turning on your husband, power should be used to help your relationship and not to dominate him. Also, unless you relieve this tension that he feels, it's going to provoke more anger from him. That is his way of dealing with stress. Because of that, during a period of calmness it's time to fill him in on what's going on.

Filling Your Husband In and Relieving His Stress

The best way to do this is face to face, but it would be good if you practice it by yourself several times before you try it with your husband. You are not going to *feel* like doing this, but don't use that as your excuse not to. In fact, you won't feel like doing any of the interventions in this book. People don't become motivated until after they start to have success, which is why many people don't make changes in the first place. But, you are becoming different, more successful. Because you know that your discomfort, and other people's discomfort, are part of the change process. Realizing this means that you are on your way to success. When you are making changes, the only things that will feel right are the things you have always done, and those things aren't working. If you are starting to think about quitting, just think about how things are and how they will continue to be if you don't make changes. Is it really easier not to change?

Arrange for him to sit down and listen to you at a quiet and calm time. Ask him not to interrupt. If he does interrupt, remind him once. If he continues to interrupt, end the conversation and try again at another time. If he gets angry and wants you to continue then and there, go back to your strategy for dealing with his anger as outlined above. The more you can stick with it, the more he will respect you, and listen to you. Respect is a very important thing to earn and you do that by being consistent. You will also earn trust by being consistently caring. He needs those things as much as you do to have a good relationship.

For many men, taking a walk together while talking works better than a sit down talk. Try both. You can also use walking and talking for the second part of your anger intervention (the five step anger follow-up).

The Messages of the Fill-In Talk

These are the messages you are going to deliver to your husband. Try not to say more than this. Saying too much causes far more problems than saying too little. He will ask questions if he wants to know more. Give him these six messages:

Message 1. You (this means you, not him) have been at fault for letting something go on too long that has been hurting your relationship with him. (It's really important that you take responsibility here. Any blaming will just set him off and accomplish nothing).

Message 2. Because you want to have a good relationship with him, you are not going to fight with him.

Message 3. You are not going to let his anger destroy your relationship with him because you *love* him (you need to say it).

Message 4. You know that most of the time, when he gets mad, it is because (and here you need to have done your homework and figured out his primary motivation) he (choose <u>one</u>) is

    a. trying to get something important done,

    b. trying to make sure something important is done the right way,

    c. trying to get along, or is

d. trying to get some appreciation for the important things he is doing.

(However you say it, be sure to use the word "important." They are important to him). Whatever motive you choose (a, b, c, or d), don't talk about it like it's a bad thing. All of these are good motives. Saying it this way helps preserve respect for him and does not give him the message that he is defective or unacceptable (East Asians would say, you are helping him to "save face").

Message 5. Tell him that when he gets mad, you will hear him out, but you won't discuss things at that time, because discussing things when he is upset makes the two of you more distant—even when he is right.

Message 6. Tell him you will discuss things with him when you are *both* calm, because it will be much easier for you to hear his important points. (By saying "both" you share the problem).

Whatever your husband says after you give him this information is not really important. It will be nice if he responds positively, but it makes no difference in terms of what you do. He doesn't have to agree, and you are not asking him to. You're also not asking him if he understands. The intervention is under your control, so it doesn't require his cooperation or understanding. He is not likely to emotionally "get it" until after things start getting better. Until then he will probably think you are very strange.

You won't be able to convince your husband to respect you or take you seriously just by talking. If you have tried to do that before, you know what I mean. But you can help him to respect you and take you seriously by being consistent and following through—every time. When you follow through, it is a wonderful learning experience for him (and you) and will literally change the nature of your relationship in a positive way.

How Long Does This Take to Work?

The more often he is angry, the *faster* this will work. That's because he will have more chances to practice (and so will you!). It's the total number of times of practice that make the most difference in changing habits and patterns. This means the worst guys change the fastest, (provided their wives are doing the interventions consistently). In severe cases, you will be able to see change in less than a week. In mild cases, it could take three to six months to change things. Why is change faster with men with severe anger problems? Actually, it has nothing to do with anger. It has to do with how people change habits. For him to change, he needs to discover that his way no longer works at all. Not 1 out of 3 times, not 1 out of 10, and not 1 out of 20. A man with severe anger problems will give you 20 chances to be consistent within a week. Therefore, he learns quickly to change. A man with occasional anger problems may need several months. It will take that long for him to have enough experiences to know that his way is just not going to work anymore. This is nothing, though, compared to years of marriage, so hang in there—it will be worth it.

Consistency, Not Severity, is the Key

Be careful, to be consistent. If you only follow through four out of five times, he will learn that his way works one out of five times. And that will maintain the behavior.

This is Not Parenting or Teaching

You are changing what *you* do when he is angry. You are not coercing him. And you are not asking him. You are not telling him what he needs to do. He will change because he chooses to, and he needs to get credit for every change he makes. You need to get credit for changing, too. But, learn to pat yourself on the back for these kinds of changes. Your reward will be a better relationship and a husband who loves you more than ever.

Things Must Get Worse Before They Can Get Better

What really helps people to keep going on any goal is seeing progress. When people don't see results right away, they often give up. The truth is, for most long term goals, you will not see positive results when you first start. A lot of the time you will actually see negative results. That is also true for the changes mentioned in this book. What successful people have learned that other people have not is that these negative results are actually a sign of progress. Let's look at an example.

When people who are out of shape start exercising, what kind of results can they expect in the first couple of weeks? Can they expect to be trim, fit, and strong? No. They can instead expect to be tired, somewhat sore, and to receive near constant messages from their brain to give up. If you know that being sore, tired, and getting urges to quit are signs that you are making good progress, you are more likely to continue. You can say to yourself, "Of course I'm sore and feel like quitting. It's because I am in the process of getting in shape. These feelings show that I am doing well. If I didn't feel sore, it would mean I'm *not* making progress." And, indeed, if you continue for a couple more weeks, you will start to feel stronger, a lot less sore, and may lose a pound or two. Keep it up for three months, and you will have a regular exercise habit, feel good, have more energy, look forward to exercising, and enjoy seeing yourself in the mirror more. Making it through the first month is the toughest part.

Now let's consider the case of changing the way you interact with your husband. As I said before, change may take 3 to 6 months of work on your part, though with a seriously angry husband you will see good results start to happen even within a week or two. Regardless of how long it takes to make the change, the course is still predictable. What can we expect to happen?

When you first start to make changes, it will feel unnatural and you will have a lot of doubts. Your husband's stress will increase, because that is a natural reaction to change. Unfortunately, since he deals with stress by becoming angry, he will become angry even more than usual. That will make you doubt what you are doing even more, since he is being even more angry than before. If you realize, however, that this pattern of doubt on your part and increased anger on your husband's part is actually a sign of progress, it can encourage you to continue. Expecting to change the way you interact with your husband without upsetting him is like expecting to get into shape without getting sore. It's just not going to happen. But, as you continue to be consistent in your interventions, he will adjust, his stress level will go down again, you will feel more comfortable doing the interventions, and his display of anger will become less intense, less prolonged, and less frequent. Keep going for three to six months and you will have a totally different pattern of interaction with your husband that will enable the two of you to be closer than ever. To put it in a briefer way—things will get worse before they get better. So, when they get worse, you can know you are on the right track.

Using a Chart to Encourage Yourself to Stick With It

There are several ways that you can chart your progress and realize that you are having success and are on the road to changing your husband. One very handy way of charting is simply to use a monthly calendar. Every time you complete another step, write it on your calendar. Remember, you are not charting your husband's anger—you are charting the changes that *you* are making to deal with his anger. On the following page is a list of steps that you can record on your calendar as you achieve them.

This chart will allow you to track your progress for at least three months. You won't need to track longer than this because after you have been consistent for three months, you will have a new habit that you will be able to easily maintain. Your husband will have learned the ineffectiveness of his anger with you and you will both have a better way of communicating than before. If you do mess up, restart your charting from day one. Your ability to sustain change is key.

If you keep a journal, you can also record this kind of information in your journal along with any positive encouragement for yourself. Don't write discouraging things in your journal, because when you

My Chart of Successes

☐ Decided to do something to improve relationship

☐ Got a book on dealing with a difficult husband

☐ Read chapter on dealing with angry husband

☐ Made this list of steps (already 4 successes!)

☐ Reviewed pattern of angry interactions and what I need to change that isn't working

☐ Decided to make the relationship a priority

☐ Responded to my husband's anger calmly by listening, restating, and scheduling

☐ Told my husband how and why I will deal with his anger (love and relationship)

☐ I have followed through without using my old method (fighting back, shutting down, etc.) for 1 day

☐ I have followed through without using my old method for 3 days in a row

☐ I have followed through without using my old method for 1 week

☐ I have followed through without using my old method for 2 weeks

☐ I have followed through without using my old method for 1 month

☐ I have followed through without using my old method for 2 months

☐ I have followed through without using my old method for 3 months

reread it, you will recreate your negative moods and doubts and you will be programming in feelings of hopelessness. Also, a journal is not a diary to mentally dump into. It's a tool for the purpose of carrying out your plan—to have a closer relationship with your husband. Only write in it what will help you to move forward.

Facing Reality is Easier Than Avoiding It

Because so many people are focused on being perfect, they often feel like things are too hard to do and so don't do them at all. I would be the same way if I thought I had to do things perfectly. When you mess up, tell yourself that it's ok, because it is. I never had a client who didn't mess up and I have never achieved a goal, myself, without messing up on something. We don't actually learn much from our mistakes, but we can learn that mistakes are par for the course. NASA messes up. Beethoven messed up. Einstein messed up. You can and will mess up, too. But, like NASA, Beethoven, and Einstein, it's important to get back on track.

The two major possibilities for things going wrong are: 1) your husband continues to be successful in pushing your buttons with his anger so you can't do the intervention; and 2) you inconsistently apply this intervention. Either one will mean that your husband's anger is still working for him. People continue to do what works some of the time. It's that "some of the time" part that we are working on taking away. Do you know any good reason why your husband's anger should work with you some of the time?

Your husband's old way (intense and frequent anger) is no longer going to work with you (thanks to you). How well will the new way work? Will it work all of the time? No way. Most of the time? Maybe. Some of the time? Yes. As long as the new way you are creating works some of the time, you will both continue using it. What this means is that if you try talking together several times and only get good results one time, that's great! Because you have both changed from your previous ways which were creating distance every time. Do you think that every meeting Microsoft has results in their creating a new product or increasing revenue? No way! The expectation that every talk we have with our spouse is going to be productive is way out of line with reality. Talk regularly. Get good results sometimes. Avoid a worse way (intense anger) all the time. That's things working well.

If All Else Fails (and even if it doesn't)

If you want extra help, get help from a local counselor for emotional support or coaching for help with the intervention. If you would like to learn more about marriage coaching or working with Coach Jack, you can visit **coachjackito.com**.

9

LOVING (AND CHANGING) THE UNHAPPY, WITHDRAWN, OR AVOIDANT MAN

Do you have a withdrawn or unhappy man? Of the three kinds of men talked about in this book, the unhappy man is the most difficult to recognize. The angry man is in your face with his anger and although you may wish that you couldn't see it, actually you can't miss it. The selfish man may hide his misbehavior for a while, but when you see it, you know it for what it is. But an unhappy, withdrawn, or avoidant man is more likely to leave you thinking, "What is going on?" "Is something wrong with him, or is something wrong with me?"

Of course, such questions are an oversimplification since the relationship always has to do with both of you. It *is* something about him, and it *is* something about you. He is doing something harmful and you are allowing it to continue. Just as with the angry man, though, this doesn't mean that you are the *cause* of either his feelings or his behavior.

Of course it is possible for your husband to become temporarily unhappy or withdrawn as a result of something you have done. But such temporary feelings are not what this chapter is all about. This chapter is about men who have made this behavior, and the moods that go along with it, their *lifestyle*—a lifestyle that is draining your relationship of love and vitality.

This chapter is not about living with men who are clinically depressed. Clinical depression is a mental and biological disorder. I will talk about it more later in this chapter so you can determine if your husband is depressed and needs to see a doctor. Rather than a depressed man, this chapter focuses on men who pull away from their partners both emotionally and physically.

If you are feeling lonely and rejected and your partner is not involved with another woman, then you probably have the kind of unhappy or withdrawn man talked about in this chapter. While *depressed* men may feel hopeless or even emotionless, they are more likely to say "I don't know what's wrong with me," than they are to say "Something is wrong with you." Perpetually unhappy and withdrawn men, on the other hand, are more likely to make you feel like you are substandard, unfixable, an irritation, or a burden on their life. They seem, for the most part, like they don't want to have anything to do with you. They are difficult men to love. They are a challenge to understand because they don't understand themselves and don't like to talk. They make you feel rejected.

Just as with the other kinds of men in this book though, these men do not want to lose their wives and are invested in their relationships. They stick around, although they are seemingly detached. If you try to break up or divorce with them, they temporarily attach more strongly. They don't want to lose their partners. Such strong attachment doesn't last when the threat of break up is gone. Therefore, threats of divorce or separation, without further action, are not an effective long term solution. This chapter will help you to change him and improve your relationship permanently. Although these men are complex, it is not as important to understand them as it is to know what to do. And you can easily learn that.

The Challenge

The challenge is not to figure him out, but to work on having an appropriate response to his behaviors which moves you both forward. You see, the emotionally avoidant man is remarkably stable in his avoidance, as long as you are. If anything is going to change in your relationship, it is going to have to start with you. Until you destabilize his world, his comfort zone, he will roll on perpetually on the same track until your relationship is over.

Another challenge with the withdrawn, avoidant, or perpetually unhappy man is maintaining feelings of love for him. In an effort to change things, at first, women often give a lot of themselves, hoping to coax the avoidant man into being more emotionally involved with them. They may be extra sweet in their talking, extra sexual or seductive, extra hard working around home, or extra sensitive in their listening. But, when they continue to get little in return, they just feel more and more drained. Their giving turns to resentment when they get little in return. Their resentment then turns to bitterness. And bitterness eventually gives way to feeling sad and hopeless. Do you recognize any of these feelings in yourself?

Loving the emotionally avoidant man is possible if you can have the perspective that he is stuck as much as you are, and that he wants to be unstuck even more than you do. But he is trapped within a web of his own habits, and the fears of his experiences. Just as an agoraphobic has learned to hide in her house, or even within one room of her house, so the emotionally withdrawn man has learned to distance with his avoidance. He wants to be a part of your world, but has too much fear to come out into it on an emotional level. If you can see that the man you love is trapped, as you are trapped, then it is easier to sympathize and love him. You will still burn out though, if you don't know what to do to help him, and may have burned out already. But even that can change.

Let me be up front with you about one thing. Your chances of success are lower with this type of man than with the other types. But if you are to save your relationship you *must* take that chance. Even partial success will result in a better life for you, end your resentment, and make you feel better about yourself, by giving you a loving way to respond to your husband, without being stuck. Allowing ourselves to come to resent our spouses for what we sacrifice "for them" is one of the worst things that we can do to a relationship. It is my hope to stop you from doing that.

Differentiate Unhappiness from Depression

One of the biggest mistakes any doctor or counselor can make is treating the wrong problem. We are biological beings and prone to many kinds of physical and emotional problems. When first helping people with severe relationship difficulties, it is prudent to first make sure that there is no contributing psychological or physical *disorder*. If there is, treating the person for that disorder should receive priority.

The kind of disorder most likely to contribute to the behaviors talked about in this chapter are mood disorders. Specifically, depression and dysthymia. They both can result in loss of interest in your relationship. If your husband is suffering from one of these disorders, the first step should be to give him information about it, so he can objectively see his symptoms and get appropriate treatment.

According to the DSM-IV-TR[11], depression requires the presence of: 1) a depressed, down, or sad mood for most of the time, more days than not, for at least a two week period; OR 2) a two week period of loss of interest or pleasure in activities that were once enjoyed. In addition to one of those two requirements, *at least four* of the following symptoms must be present *during the same two week period* for a diagnosis of depression:

1. Significant weight loss, weight gain, or change in appetite
2. Sleeping too much or too little
3. Feeling slowed down (like slow motion), physically agitated, or restless
4. Low energy; fatigue

---

[11] American Psychiatric Association: *Diagnostic and Statistical Manual of Mental Disorders*, Fourth Edition, Text Revision, Washington, DC, American Psychiatric Association, 2000.

5. Feeling worthless or excessively guilty

6. Difficulty with thinking, concentrating, or making decisions

7. Recurring thoughts of death or suicide; a suicide attempt or plan

If you are thinking that we all have some of these symptoms at times, you are right. That's why they need to occur together within a two week period. Keep in mind that *just having this information is not enough for a diagnosis because there are other qualifiers and exceptions.* But, this information should tell you enough to know whether to suspect depression or not. Assessment for depression by a professional is not difficult or painful. If depression is present, it can be treated and may be all that is needed to improve your relationship. Treatment may get your husband to the place where he is motivated to have marriage counseling, relationship coaching, or otherwise work on your relationship. However, if your husband is pretty much symptom-free except when he is with you, it is most likely not depression. The "most of the time" part of the diagnosis is an important consideration. People's biology doesn't just switch on and switch off according to who they are with. Depression would cut across much of what your husband does, whether he is with you or not.

"Dysthymia" is a little different from depression, although it is also a mood disorder. According to the DSM-IV-TR[12], dysthymia does not require as many symptoms as depression, but a depressed mood must have been present most of the time, most of the days, of at least a *two year period.* In addition, at least two of the following symptoms had to have been present, during the time when the person had the depressed mood, over that two year period:

1. Overeating or lack of appetite

2. Sleeping too much or having difficulty sleeping

3. Fatigue, lack of energy

4. Poor self-esteem

---

[12] American Psychiatric Association: *Diagnostic and Statistical Manual of Mental Disorders*, Fourth Edition, Text Revision, Washington, DC, American Psychiatric Association, 2000.

5. Difficulty with concentration or decision-making

6. Feeling hopeless

Additionally, the symptoms must also cause great distress or difficulty functioning at home, work, or other important areas. If you have the kind of man talked about in this chapter, "difficulty functioning at home" can be the severe difficulties in your relationship, provided it has been going on at least two years. Keep in mind that *just having this information is not enough for a diagnosis because there are other qualifiers and exceptions.* However, this information should tell you enough to know whether to suspect dysthymia or not. Sometimes when people have had dysthymia for many years, it just seems normal to them. Being treated and recovering from this disorder may help them to get out of an emotion dampening fog they have been living in, and out into a bright and exciting world.

I offer this information here, not as your resource for information about these disorders, but merely to allow you to quickly assess whether your husband *may* be suffering from a mood disorder. If you think that may be the case, your next step is to get more information from an official source like NIMH.[13] Remember, "When in doubt, check it out."

The rest of this chapter is written with the assumption that your husband is *not* suffering from an untreated mood disorder, although he may have some of the same symptoms.

Looking Closely at the Motivations Behind Your Husband's Distance or Withdrawal

Trying to understand your withdrawn or avoidant husband can be a frustrating experience. It's easy to conclude that he is not interested in having a close relationship, or at least in not having a close relationship with you. After all, if you were not interested in

---

[13] The National Institute of Mental Health (NIMH) is part of The National Institutes of Health (NIH), a component of the U.S. Department of Health and Human Services. You can find them on the web at: www.nimh.nih.gov.

having a close relationship with someone, you might behave in the same way—making promises without keeping them, seeming disinterested when they invite you to do something together, and canceling dates at the last minute. If you really did have a lack of interest in your partner, what would happen after a while? Wouldn't you start to become interested in someone else? This is typically *not* the case with the withdrawn husband.

A withdrawn man is typically not trying to have a close relationship with someone else. I don't mean that he's not *tempted* to have an affair with someone, but remember that temptations and plans are very different. If he became involved with another woman, he is likely to eventually behave with her much the same way as he does now with you. His withdrawal is more his way of having a relationship than it is *because* of your relationship. This kind of man can go through several relationships, staying with a woman until she gets burned out with his avoidance and then move on to the next. It is likely that your withdrawn or avoidant man has had such committed-yet-distant relationships before. If your husband is in his first committed relationship, he is likely to have had such distance within his family of origin. This behavior doesn't just come from nowhere.

The reason to assume that the issue is with your husband and not with you is simple. When people have experienced closeness in their previous relationships, they like it and become dissatisfied with distance. Such people may temporarily use distance to avoid conflict, but they don't like it. They are motivated to become close again and will try to do that even if it results in severe conflict. If conflict is prolonged, they will withdraw for a while or even end the relationship—so that they can have a close relationship again.

Your husband is likely to be distant and avoidant for one of two reasons: 1) he has never had a close relationship and is comfortable being independent; or 2) he is distancing himself not so much from you, but from an issue in your relationship that he sees as unchangeable. I call the first kind of man "comfortably distant" and the second kind of man "miserably distant" to reflect how they feel.

Interventions for these two types of men are a little different, so I will talk about them separately.

The motivation of the *comfortably* distant man is to remain comfortable—to maintain his distance and to react to threats against it. If you have such a man, he *does* need you and *does* desire the relationship. That is why he is committed to you. But, he is as close as he wants to be. He will work on changing only when things become uncomfortable, so that must be *part* of your strategy in changing him. Simply making him uncomfortable though (for example by nagging), will just increase his desire to distance himself from you. Besides feeling uncomfortable, he will also need to experience a more satisfying resolution to his discomfort than his usual distancing. I will teach you how to help him do that.

The motivation of the *miserably* distant man is to avoid conflict or wait for a time when he can have a new partner. Because he doesn't believe that your relationship issues can be resolved or are not worth the bother, he puts more energy into avoiding interacting with you than he does in working things out with you. His behavior is designed to also convince you of the hopelessness of working on the relationship so that you will leave him alone. Although unhappy with the relationship, if he can avoid it well enough and have some small pleasures in his life, he may be able to live this way indefinitely. In the end, he will feel resentful—like he has been cheated out of a better life. Any partner who stayed committed to him would also end up with the same feeling. The strategy for changing this kind of man is to increase his discomfort level so that his avoidance does not work, while also making a way for him to have what he really wants but believes he cannot have—a closer relationship with you.

Both types of men are similar in that they would both enjoy having a close relationship with their partner, if they could only experience it. This means that no matter which of these motivators your husband has, he both needs you and would enjoy a close relationship with you. When you deal successfully with the avoidant, distant, detached man, you end up with a close partner.

Make Sure Your Own Neediness Doesn't Get in the Way of Change

Do you need your husband to change in order for you to be happy? If so, you are dealing from a position of weakness and inequality. He can maintain power over you just by refusing to change, since you need him to in order to be happy. Your neediness can even provide the motivation for your husband not to change, because it gives him a kind of power, a feeling of control, that he may not have in other areas of his life. If he has a grudge against you, being distant can also be his way of giving you what he believes you deserve.

On the other hand, if you don't need your husband to change in order for you to be happy, it takes away all power and punishment motive on his part. It makes the playing field equal. His thinking will become like this—"You want to spend time with me, and if I don't spend time with you, you will spend your time elsewhere. So, if I don't spend time with you, I risk losing you." A withdrawn man wouldn't fear losing a *needy* woman and would have little reason to consider her needs. Her neediness would make it less likely that she would get what she needed. Her neediness would guarantee her unhappiness.

Being needy would not give you the position of strength that you need to help your partner out of his withdrawn or avoidant position. There's only one way in which you ideally should "need" your husband. You should need his cooperation in order to have a good *relationship* with him. But, that is not the same thing as needing him to cooperate in order for you to be happy. Your happiness should not depend on the actions or inactions of your husband. It gives him way too much control, and puts him at the center of blame if you are not happy. You are the master controller of your life and happiness—not your husband.

Part of successfully changing the avoidant or withdrawn man will be your becoming as self sufficient as possible both physically and emotionally. You need to become more self-sufficient before you can become close. You want to be at the place where you can honestly say:

"I have a good life going on here. I want you to be a part of it and I want to share it with you. Then, we can really have an enjoyable relationship. But, if you choose not to, then I am going to keep moving ahead with my life. I am not closing the door on you, but I am not going to stay locked on the inside of the door with you. We can be happy together, or you can be miserable by yourself."

A needy woman could not possibly say that sincerely. She would not have the strength that she needs to help both herself and her husband out of this situation. She would be too afraid of his leaving her. Her neediness would prevent her from doing anything effective, and so eventually she would get the result she fears.

The chances are that you *are* a needy person and that is part of your predicament now. The good news is that you can stop being needy. This is often part of what I work on with my clients. Your neediness did not cause your husband to be this way (or any other way). Many needy women have husbands who are not this way. But, your neediness will make it difficult for you to change your partner because he is this way. Overcoming your neediness is the first step to changing your husband and getting respect. It must be done *before* you do the direct interventions aimed at changing him. *Otherwise, they won't work.* If ever you needed a reason not to be needy, you have it now. If you have children, your overcoming your neediness will also teach them not to be needy and prevent them from becoming trapped in a future relationship they feel helpless to change.

This is not a chapter on overcoming neediness, but you will benefit from having some idea of what it means to not be needy. It means that you have the physical means to support yourself (usually having to do with money), as well as close family or friends who do things with you, make you feel important, and give you emotional support. It means that if your husband were to vanish from the face of the earth, you would miss him, but you would not be in a desperate situation either emotionally or physically. People who have such assurance can freely give and receive love and can communicate easily about anything. They still have boundaries—in fact very good boundaries—because they don't compromise their values. They are loved, respected, and treated as equals.

Needy people experience intense love at the beginning of their relationships, with either a gradual decline in love or a roller coaster like cycling of closeness and distance. People who are not needy, have a more stable love that grows with sharing over the lifetime of the relationship. People who transition from their neediness can also have such stable, secure love. Start putting into your life today what you would need if you were not with your husband (this does not mean finding another man who will take care of your needs!). You don't need to match his income or resources to be equal. You just need to be in a position to be able to take care of yourself both physically and emotionally. If you need professional guidance to do that (for example from a coach), then get it. Why? For the sake of the relationship you have right now with your husband as well as your future happiness.

Changing Your Husband's Behavior

As stated above, if you are a needy person, the first thing that will go on your plan is overcoming your neediness so that you can effectively change your husband. You don't need to be more powerful than your husband, but you do need to be able to take care of yourself so you can help him to change. Take as much time as you need to make this happen. Everything else depends on it.

Assuming that you are not needy, or have overcome your neediness, what comes next? Well, since you are not needy, you have a social support network, enough savings to be able to take of yourself for at least a few months, and have activities that you enjoy on a regular basis. This makes your life, in comparison to your husband's, seem rather good. Although he may be avoiding you, he is not having nearly as good a time as you. And any kind of control that he may have had over you by avoiding you, is now gone. What is that you say? That is not where you are? Well, that is where your plan needs to take you. Your husband is not stopping you from doing those things. Although he may not like it, may tell you not to, may make a lot of noise, he is actually not stopping you from having an enjoyable life (with the exception of an enjoyable relationship with him). Misery *does* love company, but miserable company is no fun. What you are doing is not selfish in the least because you will be inviting him to join you at every point. Only he can keep himself miserable.

An Intervention for the Emotionally Avoidant, *Satisfied* Man

If your husband is avoiding you because that is his natural style, not knowing how to have a closer relationship, your having a life of your own and enjoying yourself is going to be alien to him. In his lifetime, he will not have seen that in a relationship. Other women he was with probably were content to be miserable, complaining, or "patient" until they finally ended their relationship with him. After which, they may have created a happier life, but in all probability just recreated the same situation with another man and are living miserably somewhere else today. You, by learning to enjoy your own life and moving ahead on such things as career, friends, and personal goals *while still in your relationship* with your husband, is something that he won't know how to deal with.

If you improved your life and moved forward without his participation or cooperation, it would be hard for the both of you. To make it easier, you will give him choices at each step of the way. These choices will show him your desire to be close to him and to have a better relationship with him, but your unwillingness to remain miserable or "stuck" with him. For example, suppose that your husband never goes out with you. He may *agree* to do things with you, but finds excuses not to follow through—teaching you not to ask him in the future about doing things together. If you recognize that you have already learned this, you can see that he has effectively changed you. To turn that situation around, make back up plans to go out with one of your friends if your husband doesn't follow through.

Example Statements to Prepare a Backup Plan

(You to your friend): *"I want to go out with my husband this weekend, but he usually refuses or backs out. Would you be willing to go out with me if my husband backs out?"*

(You to your husband): *"I would really like to go out with you this weekend. You can choose the activity, I just want to be with you and have a good time. If you can't though, I won't insist. I will just go out with one of my friends instead."*

After this, you either go out with your husband or your friend. Under no circumstances do you stay home. This is the basic method: show your desire to be with your husband, but be unwilling to be kept on a shelf. And even if he cancels at the last minute, do not complain. Notice that there is nothing sneaky, dishonest, rejecting, or manipulative about this. Your husband has a free choice without any kind of bad results for himself whichever way he chooses. Notice, however, that he gets to choose the activity. That is an incentive, but it is also a way for you to show you want to be with him. It is a very positive message. Later, we will talk about how to behave with him when he does follow through and go out with you.

For other aspects of your life that you are working on, also try to invite his involvement, include him when possible, and present an incentive. For example, when deciding to get a new job, you can invite his help and provide an incentive for him to do so. Note, however, that you are *not ever* asking his permission to improve your life. That is what a needy person would do, but that is not you, right? You don't need his permission to improve your life, do you?

A Sample Statement for Inviting Participation

(You to your husband): "I have decided to get a job doing something I like. I would really like your help with this. If we work together, we can also create a budget for saving for that boat you have been wanting. But, if you don't want to help, that's ok. I can work on it by myself and decide by myself how the money should be used."

Again, it's the same basic method. An invitation with an incentive, with no pressure, and with a backup plan that is good for you.

If you routinely follow this method, he will feel more and more left out, but also not be able to blame you for that. The result is that he will start to take you up on your invitation to participate. At first, he will probably refuse or change his mind at the last minute, hoping that you will, too. But, when you follow through with your back-up plan, he will quickly learn that either he participates or he gets left out. Add to that his underlying fear of your leaving him, and he is more likely to follow through the next time. This approach is the "crowbar" that will pry him away from his usual avoidance activities—even if those avoidance activities are taking place outside your home (bars, golf course, working extra hours, etc.).

With this method, patience and persistence are important. There is no place for nagging and complaining. These just decrease his desire to be with you and work against you. You will find that even if your husband does not want to do things with you most of the time, that you become less resentful and more comfortable with him when you are together. He may never become the social butterfly that you might be, but he will enjoy being with you sometimes. The more he learns to like it, the less resistant he will be to increased togetherness. Sometimes this is all that is needed to revitalize a relationship.

Understanding the Emotionally Avoidant, *Dissatisfied* Man

The emotionally avoidant, dissatisfied man is not avoidant because he wants to be. It is *not* his preferred style of living, although it is one of his preferred ways of coping with relationship difficulties. This makes him very different from the avoidant, satisfied man.

Being dissatisfied, he is not motivated to continue to avoid. On the contrary, he wants a very different way of living—perhaps even more than you do. But, because he doesn't believe that it's possible for him to create that situation with you, he is either waiting for you to somehow change to suit him, or he is waiting for some way out of the relationship. It is also quite possible that he is waiting for either one, with no big preference either way. He just knows for sure that he does not like his relationship with you the way it is now. As bad as that may sound, it is actually common ground for the two of you, because you don't like the way things are either. You both feel like martyrs.

Unlike the avoidant satisfied man, the avoidant dissatisfied man has had a close relationship (with you at another time or with someone else) and he would like very much to have that again. We don't miss what we haven't had, but he has had it. If you were satisfied with his avoidance, it would be a very frustrating situation for him. On the other hand, if you are unhappy with the relationship, it means you are more likely to change the way you are, or that you are more likely to leave the relationship. So you can see why he's not motivated to make you happy. The dissatisfied man usually prefers his wife to make changes that he wants, and that's one reason he sticks around. He will take the second choice of leaving if necessary, but it takes time for him to be ready for that, especially as he gets older.

A big part of creating change with the dissatisfied man will *not* be randomly doing things to try to make him feel satisfied. Many women try this strategy of doing many different things that they think please men. When they do have some success, it is usually temporary, and in the end, a frustrating experience. Men are rarely distant because what they want is a better dinner, a romantic evening, or a new fishing rod. Men who are upset about such things act more like whiny spoiled children than they do like avoidant men.

For avoidant men, there is a much bigger issue. You may know exactly what it is and may be avoiding it yourself. If so, this is a kind of collusion, where you are both silently agreeing to avoid the real issue. He wants something you don't and neither of you is willing to budge. The result is distance. It is a waiting game whose length depends on the patience or stubbornness of the players.

It is possible, though, that you may not know what he wants. Finding out will be important. Currently he is afraid and unwilling to say what it is, or he doesn't even know himself. Why would a man be unwilling to say what he wants if he thinks it is the only way to have a good relationship, or the only way that he can be happy? There are a few major reasons: 1) he may be afraid of being rejected because living on his own may be more difficult than living with you; 2) he probably believes that you would never agree with what he wants and bringing it up would just create more stress; or 3) he may be afraid of emotionally hurting you. He may believe that coming out in the open with what he wants would just cause conflict and make things even worse. His avoidance, after all, is a way of coping—of avoiding stress. He might give it up if he really thought he could get something better, but he is unlikely to give it up if he thinks it will create a more stressful situation.

If you don't know what he wants, you really can't assure him that you will either help him to have it or that you won't be upset by it. In fact, you may have the same fear in finding out that he has in telling you. These "matching" fears are very common in relationships and keep people stuck. Since he is not about to change his beliefs and open up to you on his own, it will be up to you to change how you deal with him. Just putting up with avoidance day after day (or night after night), is itself a kind of avoidance. Getting unstuck will require a forward looking perspective.

An Intervention for the Avoidant, Dissatisfied Man

Hopefully, you are sick and tired of living the way you are with this kind of man. It's got to be more scary to think about continuing to live in this situation than your fear of what might happen when you start to make changes. Besides thinking what it would be like to be stuck in this situation for years, consider the possibility that your husband's "solution" of somehow exiting the relationship may come along any day now. What is he waiting for? Another woman? More money? A new job in a different city? I have no idea and neither do you. But, that really doesn't matter. Because reacting to his solution won't be helpful. Your best solution will be to take action before he is ready to. That will precipitate a crisis, shake things up, and pull the avoidance rug out from under his feet. That's far better than waiting for him to do that to you because you will do it for the sake of the relationship.

While it sounds like you are getting ready to do something *to* your husband, keep in mind that what you are actually doing is getting ready to do something *for* your husband. Here is the mindset to have—"If what he really needs to be happy is within my power, I will help him to get it." As simple as that. With that mindset, you will be able to talk to him, both on the same side, without conflict. You may risk losing the relationship if what he wants is not good for your relationship, but to oppose him would result in greater distance, or stalemate at best. The only way to hold onto a man who is unhappy with your relationship is to work with him to help him get what he wants. Helping him to do that pulls him closer in a way that fighting about differences never would. You must temporarily set your relationship concerns aside in order to ultimately keep it. You must for the moment concern yourself with what *he* is concerned with.

So how do you get started? First, let me tell you a couple of things not to do. Don't start by telling him you are unhappy with your relationship. That kind of self-focus won't help. And don't start by telling him that he is not happy (although it is most likely true), as he won't like your "mind reading." Instead, start with the simple truth that this kind of relationship is not what you signed up for and you don't think it is what he had in mind either. If you are wrong, and he really does like this kind of relationship, then you have an avoidant, *satisfied* man. Otherwise, you will be right. Then, tell him that you have been making a mistake to let it go on so long, because it is not helping either of you to get what you want. His anxiety should really start to build, because it is ahead of schedule for him. Tell him that you would really like to know what he wants so that you can help him get it. But, don't insist. Whether he shares what he wants or not, tell him you are planning to move forward with your life.

Example Statement to the Avoidant, Dissatisfied Man

(You to your husband): "Bob, our relationship doesn't seem to be going the way we planned when we got married. I'm sorry I didn't say something sooner. I would really like to help you have the kind of future you want. If you don't want to share with me what that is, that's ok, but I'm going to move forward with my life."

If he has no response at this time, that is ok. He is probably in kind of an internal panic state. Walk away and get about your plan to improve your life, just as a woman with an avoidant, *satisfied* man would. Your making changes in your life will be the force that changes him. It won't work for him to be avoidant anymore, because you will no longer be waiting for him. He has either got to fish or cut bait. If he is working on an exit plan, he may try to convince you that he is really interested in your relationship, in an effort to buy time. You can put this response to the test by asking him to get counseling or coaching with you. There is also a very good chance that at some point he will verbally attack you about how you are such a bad partner and how he has been stuck in this miserable relationship long enough. That's a predictable and ok thing to happen, because we are about to prepare for it. You will be able to put his reaction to good use.

Dealing with a Verbal Attack After Your Intervention

Prepare to be blamed for anything and everything. The main purpose of such an attack will be for him to justify his behavior and to regain control. Now that you are taking action, by being financially and emotionally independent, he has lost control—control that he had before just by avoiding you. He is not going to want to have counseling with you. Having counseling would be a problem solving approach and the exact opposite of his normal avoidance approach.

The best way to deal with his attack is, like a judo artist, not to counter his attack, but to go with it. Agree with him that he is unhappy about many things and that things really do need to change. He is right. Things do need to change. You want something different for your future, and so does he. Get on his side about that. Agree with him that you really may not be the woman who can help him to get what he wants, because you are not even sure what he wants (true enough, isn't it?). Although what he said about you in his attacks may be totally false, the main goal here is to get on his side about wanting something different for the future. It is what you two have in common. It is the point of connection from which the relationship can build.

It may sound like this way leads directly to divorce, but it doesn't. In joining him, you can begin to talk for real, maybe for the first time in years. Your mutual dissatisfaction gives you something to agree on without the tension of trying to force the relationship to work. From here, you can go for walks together, talking about what you really want for the future. If you are very needy, his desires for the future will trigger your jealousy and insecurity about being abandoned and you will focus on your needs, becoming very angry in the process. But, if you are not needy, you will start to see what he really needs and wants in his life. Understanding him better will help the both of you.

163

From here, you can work together to help each other to get the life that you both want to have (even if it is a separate life from each other). The very process of working together will help you to *attach* to each other. Somewhere in the process, you may surprisingly find that you have the best sex together that you have had in years. Working together to help each other, without selfishness, and without insecurity will build your relationship. Even the common goal of working on being separate can help a couple to become closer together! The typical way people become separate is by fighting about differences, which creates more distance. You can't fight your way to a closer relationship.

Some years ago, I saw a scene in a movie where a teenage boy was kicking the side of his coach's van, denting it in. The coach had been trying to emotionally reach this boy, but the boy had always resisted him. The more the coach tried to get close to the boy, the angrier the boy got. He just knew that he couldn't let this coach into his heart. What did the coach do when he saw the boy kicking in the side of his van? He got along side of him, and started to also kick in the side of his own van. He joined in with the boy's anger about how much life wasn't fair. It was the connection that they needed to start to build their relationship.

This book was written to help you with really hard core difficult men. These men don't respond well to requests for counseling or talking things through. They require tough, but loving interventions. You must either do them or let the relationship go. Things won't change just by doing more of the same or by being patient. The loving thing to do is to be tough, but honest, fair, and caring, without being deceptive. I don't believe that relationships can be promoted with dishonesty or without love.

Let's review the steps involved in this intervention for the avoidant, dissatisfied man:

Step 1. Point out the obvious that the relationship is not the way either of you want it to be.

Step 2. State your unwillingness to just let it continue to harm the both of you.

Step 3. Start to work on changes for yourself (more friends, social activities, part-time work, savings, etc.) that help you to be emotionally and financially secure.

Step 4. Wait for his reaction while you are doing this. It may take a while for him to be convinced that you are really changing.

Step 5a. *If he has an apologetic reaction*, do not attack him. Get to work on talking about the kind of future that he wants to have. This may be an opening for couple's counseling or couple's coaching. Or it may be his stalling for time.

Step 5b. *If he has a verbally attacking reaction*, agree with him about wanting a different future. Don't defend yourself. Continue to have talks about it and how you can help each other with what you really want to have, even if you can't get it from each other.

Step 6. Continue to work on your self-change to prevent a falling back into the old pattern.

Step 7. Continue to help each other with the futures that you both want to have. Don't be afraid of this leading to divorce. Working together is one of the most powerful things you can do to save your relationship.

Troubleshooting

It's not necessary to anticipate all potential problems—just the major ones. Doing that, and preparing for them, maximizes your chances of success.

Problem #1. <u>Neediness</u>. Dare I go over the neediness problem again? I think not. But, it is the major thing that could go wrong. Be sure to deal with this first, before attempting to do an intervention with your husband. Get professional help with this because time is not on your side.

Problem #2. <u>Your husband leaves</u>. If this happens, it will be because he was on the verge of leaving anyhow. There is nothing in this intervention worth leaving about for a man who is satisfied with the relationship. There is no way to prevent this possibility, since not working on change would also result in his leaving. In general, the longer you wait, the greater the risk of his leaving. All the more important that you be able to survive on your own for a few months if he does.

Problem #3. <u>Your husband instantly improves</u>. Enjoy it, take advantage of it, but remember that instant improvement doesn't result in permanent change. Keep following through with your self changes. Most likely he won't stay improved for long. If so it's not a sign that your method is not working. On the contrary, it's a sign that it is.

Problem #4. <u>Nothing happens</u>. If you are really making changes in your life, this is virtually impossible. I have only seen this when people *thought* they were making significant changes, but in actuality were doing very little. Others can't see your changes in *thinking* or improvement in *understanding*. That's why simply understanding things does not result in changing others. And that's why getting your husband to understand you also does not result in change. Rather than his understanding, it is your behavior of moving toward a desired goal that creates change. You cannot grow a garden simply by understanding how plants grow or by getting someone else to understand. Actions like planting seeds, watering, etc., are what really create change and growth. So too, do actions in your relationship.

Problem #5. <u>You become afraid he will leave</u>. If he has withdrawn from you, he already has emotionally left you. This method is for getting him back. If you simply want him to be under your roof, even though he is disconnected from you, then you don't need this intervention at all. Just work on yourself while you get used to not having a relationship with him. I think this would be the hardest choice of all and not what this method is about. Remember, working on yourself needs to be combined with love, openness, invitation, and helping. Those things don't work when done separately, but they work wonderfully when done together.

The Unhappy Man

Another kind of difficult man, with features similar to the withdrawn man, is the unhappy man. As I said earlier, I am not talking about the depressed man. The depressed man needs psychological and/or psychiatric help. However, even after he gets such help, he may still present himself as an unhappy man and then the techniques in this chapter will be helpful for you.

There are things that you can do that will help an unhappy man to do better. First, you will need to manage how you think about your husband's unhappiness, lack of energy, or lack of desire to do things. He is different from the relationally withdrawn man because he both wants to be close to you and is not blaming you for his problems. He probably sees rather realistically, that his own lack of enthusiasm and energy make the relationship less enjoyable for you. Knowing that probably contributes even more to his unhappiness. The best way to see him is as he actually is, without going beyond that. In other words, don't overthink or overanalyze him. "Figuring him out" is not going to change anything, because even if you could understand perfectly why he is the way that he is, you would still have exactly the same situation.

Rather than working on understanding him, it will be your job to do two things: 1) not become codependent for his thinking and behavior; and 2) become more active while encouraging more activity from him. If you sit around waiting for him to initiate some change in your relationship, you will become as resentful as wives of other difficult husbands. That won't help him or you. Arguing won't energize him either, as he is likely to use it as evidence that things really are as bad as he says and soon you will be believing it too. Your becoming an unhappy woman will not at all help him. You will need to work on becoming the opposite from him. You will need to work on becoming active and involved in your life. Your moving in this direction will help to move him in that direction, too. You can't push an unhappy man into action, but you can lead him into action. Why is action so important? Because action elevates mood. Because action gives us something positive to focus on. And because action changes outcomes.

One of the reasons the unhappy man is in this chapter with the emotionally withdrawn man is because your intervention is similar to what wives of withdrawn men must do. The message that he needs to get from your actions are, "I love you, but I am not going to sit around and wait for you to overcome your unhappiness. I am going to create a life that interests me and makes me happy. I will invite you to be a part of everything, but I'm not going to give it up if you refuse." Although that may seem cold, it is actually the most powerful thing that you can do to help him out of his unhappiness and to a better life. He can't do it on his own. And your sitting around wouldn't help.

When he sees you going out, working on projects, and doing things with your friends, he might become angry or jealous. But, you are going to head that off by regularly inviting him, urging him to go with you, to help you with your project, to meet your friend, to take that trip with you, etc. At first, he will refuse, but as you become less available for him and less codependent for his behaviors, his need for you will grow. Your refusal to sit around will mean that in order for him to get his emotional needs met, he is going to have to get off that couch and go do something with you, even if he doesn't feel like it.

When he does go with you, it will be time for you to give him a lot of love and attention. If he goes to see a friend with you, brag about him to your friend in front of him by saying honest things that he's proud of. Don't say anything negative about him to others. Although you may really want to talk with him a lot when he goes out with you, hold back. Encourage him to talk. Ask his opinion about things and don't work to cheer him up or argue with him. If he wants to talk about government corruption on your walk, listen to him. Focus on the fact that he is being active and talking to you. That's a big step. The content of his talking will change over time, as he becomes more involved in things.

When people sit around, the only things they have to talk about are what they hear on the news and replays of what they have said, done, and experienced before. When he first becomes active with you, this is all he will have. As you do more together, he will develop interests around activities. At first, he may only like to do one of your many activities with you. It can become your weekly routine to do at least one thing together.

Above all, remember that misery loves company. That's good if you don't sit around being miserable with him, as he will go out or do things with you just for the company. If you do sit around with him, he will already have the company and have absolutely no reason (from his perspective), to do anything except to complain about life.

If you are asking, "Why do I need to become so active, if he's not?" I can give you three reasons: 1) so that you don't use your husband as an excuse for your own unhappiness; 2) so that your husband will have opportunities for increased activity; and 3) so that you are not needy and resentful because you don't have a more positive, interactive, or giving husband. Neediness kills relationships. Resentment does the same. The less needy you are, the more you can "activate" both your own happiness and your husband's, and the less likely you are to become resentful.

Troubleshooting Your Intervention with the Unhappy Man

Problem #1. <u>He refuses to participate with you</u>. It is inevitable that he will refuse as first, because nothing has really changed in his environment. Although you may have planned activities, you have either not done them yet, or done them very little. For him, it is just a temporary discomfort to have you gone. He may see this as selfishness on your part—you are having a good time, while he is at home being miserable. He will see things this way because he will not yet be aware that it is he who is keeping himself feeling miserable. He will need to become more uncomfortable (actually, more needy) before he will be willing to do what is uncomfortable for him—namely, to join you. Just keep working on your life. The beginning is always the hardest. But after a while, you will enjoy your involvement in life, and so become better at involving your husband in it.

Problem #2. <u>He says your lack of caring is ruining your relationship</u>. He may actually feel that way. From his perspective, your behavior is pretty uncaring. Children who are sent off to their first day of school often have the same feeling—"Why is she abandoning me?" Healthy interventions with people who have unhealthy behavior feel bad to them at first. See his resistance as a sign of your progress. A lack of such resistance means that either your husband is not really unhappy and inactive, or that you are not really getting out and getting involved with life.

Problem #3. <u>You don't know how to become more involved with life</u>. It is quite possible that you have been so uninvolved with life for so long, that you are rusty at it. Or, you may have never been much of a participant. In either case, you may need to get help in making some goals for your future and getting to work on them. A coach is an excellent choice for such a venture, since coaches emphasize action as a way of changing and progressing.

Problem #4. (Worst case scenario). <u>You develop a very healthy life which you enjoy and which is leading toward your future goals, but your husband still refuses any kind of involvement with you</u>. Although this is not likely—unless he is suffering from an untreated depression—it is possible. You will have more choices and more leverage than you would have if you did not develop your own life. You also won't be resentful, but probably just feeling sorry for your husband who is cheating himself out of a richer life and relationship. You may want to get help from a marriage coach who specializes in reconciliation to do a stronger intervention at this point. Consulting with a marriage coach can also help you make sure that you are really at the point where a higher level of intervention is necessary.

Preventing Relapse To Withdrawal and Unhappiness

Preventing a recurrence of withdrawal really depends on making sure that it no longer works for your husband. It worked for him before, and that's why he did it for so long. When he gets stressed in the future (everyone gets stressed at times), he is going to have the same tendency to withdraw.

Don't freak out when you see that he needs some time for himself. Every man does. Having space is a normal way of coping with stress for men. If you see that happen, don't automatically assume that he is withdrawing. You can think of it more as recharging. Let him recharge.

The main way to prevent recharging from becoming withdrawal is for you to continue to participate in life, your activities, and your goals. If you start to shut down when you see him shutting down, then he will shut down all the more and you will have a return to baseline.

"Does This Method Mean I Always Have to Be On the Go?"

Not at all. You only need to be "on the go" to the extent that you *want to* be active and to the extent that you have goals you *want to* achieve in life. You may also need your own recharge time. Take it. The biggest mistake you can make is to wait for your husband to change so that you can really enjoy your life. With a withdrawn, distant, or perpetually unhappy husband, your behavior needs to be the opposite of his. Focus on enjoying your life and then your husband will become less withdrawn and more involved with you. He will only sit around and wait if you do.

Using a Chart to Encourage Yourself to Stick With It

As with the other interventions in this book, they become more effective the longer you persist. You can expect little or no response at first as your husband "waits out" your changes. Then you can expect his anger when you don't fall back into the pattern that he is used to (at that point, you will have gained control over the situation, and he will have lost it). Then, as you persist, his behavior will change, resulting in a new pattern for both of you—a better one.

The best way to fail is to give up too early and the best way to succeed is to persist until you get lasting change. You will need some ways to encourage yourself along the way. I suggest making a checklist of progress something like the one on the next page.

An End To Hopelessness

As a reminder, this is not your garden variety advice for your friend who is having a little difficulty with her husband. These interventions are specifically for the really tough men who are not motivated to work on their relationships and who are not about to change unless they "have to." These methods are positive in that they always invite your husband to become closer to you, while putting an end to the destruction caused by his behavior. The most hopeless situations are ones in which you don't know what to do and don't get help. Or when you believe your only option is ending the relationship.

If you don't know what to do or need extra help, get it. It's as simple as that. There are many family therapists and coaches like myself who are helping people to change their difficult relationships to close relationships. Just do as much as you can and then get help from there. Soon you will be able to do more and more without help. Maybe one day, you'll be helping others to enjoy their relationship, too.

If you would like to learn more about getting marriage coaching, you can visit **coachjackito.com**.

172

Checklist of Progress

☐ Wrote out my goals for career, living, personal, and social

☐ Made plans that I can work on instead of waiting for my relationship to become better

☐ Started to make changes (create a separate list of changes), such as getting a new job, making a new friend, renewing contacts with old friends, joining a club, starting a hobby, etc.

☐ Saw my husband's anger as a sign that I was making progress, and as an opportunity to communicate about what we both really want

☐ Began inviting my husband to participate and do activities with me, starting with small things such as going for a walk, helping in the garden, going out for coffee, etc.

☐ Started helping my husband in pursuing his interests so that he wouldn't feel stuck and so that I would become more valuable to him

☐ Did not take his refusal personally—just as an indication that I need to keep working on my life

☐ Continued to invite my husband to do things with me, always having back-up plans in case he refused

☐ Gave my husband attention and made him feel important when he did things with me

"A man usually values that most for which he has labored; he uses that most frugally which he has toiled hour by hour and day by day to acquire." Dorothea Dix

10

LOVING (AND CHANGING) THE SELFISH MAN

Do you have a selfish man? A selfish man tries to get something for himself, at the expense of your relationship. He is so focused on taking care of himself, that it feels like he doesn't care about you or what you want. If you ask him to share his time, money, sexual satisfaction, or any other thing, he will react with defensiveness and anger. He will treat you as though you are the selfish one who doesn't care about him.

The Challenge

The challenge in loving and changing the selfish man is to get him to make a conscious choice between your relationship and those things which are harming your relationship. Until now, he has been able to have both. There are very harsh ways to force such choices, such as threatening to divorce or breakup. But threatening to divorce or breakup comes across as controlling and often as selfish. Just making threats gives the message, "My needs are more important than your needs." Such messages increase conflict without making closer relationships. People who start out making threats, no matter how well they intend, often end up carrying out those threats with regret. Never threaten to do what you don't want to do. If you don't follow through, you will lose respect. If you do follow through, you will have regrets.

The interventions you will learn in this chapter are different from threats. They communicate choices rather than make demands. And they put the good of the relationship first. None of the interventions are needy or desperate, and they don't reject your husband. They will surprise him and be different from what he has experienced before. They won't give him a chance to argue about anything. In fact, your interventions will help him as much as you. As his partner, you are more than willing to help him get what he needs and wants and to do what you can to save the relationship. But you will only do it in a way that is good for both of you. This is both the message and the opportunity you will give him when you do the interventions in this chapter. Because the way you say things is important, the examples in this chapter will help you to know exactly what to say.

Another facet of these interventions is that they start our gently and increase in firmness, as necessary. Using a harsh intervention when one is not needed can be damaging. But, it is also damaging, and potentially relationship-ending, to not use a harsh intervention when one is needed. We must sometimes amputate a limb to save a life, but we try less drastic measures first. As always, I will not encourage you to use divorce or breakup as an intervention. I will instead teach you the three levels of intervention my clients use to save their marriages, prevent separation, breakup, and divorce.

Understanding His Selfishness

We all have many things in our life that we value. We value time with friends, our health, our families, our activities, our money, our homes, and so on. We don't want to lose any of them. We only willingly give up something we value in order to get or keep something else that we value more. We will give up free time to go to work because we need an income to survive. We give up dating others in order to have a committed relationship with our partner. We donate money to charity because we value what the charity does. We can make such decisions because we have an internal hierarchy of values. Everyone has a different hierarchy and some of our values come into conflict with those of others.

Our own values can also be in conflict. When that happens, we often compromise. We value our health very highly and would give up most other things to keep it. We would give up almost everything to save our life. But, we would give up our own life to save a loved one's life. Some of our compromises are less noble. We may, for example, let our health deteriorate a bit, as we enjoy high fat foods or watch hours of television. We may shortchange our sleep and even our relationships as we try to get more of something else. The more we compromise something we value, the greater our risk of losing it. We can lose our health, our friends, our relationships, our jobs, and even our lives if we compromise too much.

The selfish man does value his relationships, but he more readily compromises these relationships to please himself. He *underestimates* the risk of losing his relationships and harms them in the process. Here is both your key to understanding him and to changing him. It explains why he poorly judges what is harmful behavior. Interventions must get him to more accurately see the risk to his relationship.

Most of us learn as children that when we take turns and share our toys, it promotes our relationships with others. It helps us to make friends who will also share their toys as well as play with us. So, even if we are temporarily deprived of something, what we get in return (the friendship) is more valuable. As we grow older, we learn that taking turns and sharing lead to more and better relationships. This is true not only in our private and social lives, but in our professional lives as well.

Unfortunately, not everyone learns the benefits of sharing and reciprocity. This can happen when children do not learn to share or only learn to minimally share. Children without siblings or playmates may get used to whatever they need being provided for them. They may not learn the joy of providing for others. Well meaning parents who wish to provide everything for their children, without making any demands of them, can sometimes raise very selfish children who later become selfish adults. Although such selfish adults are responsible for their behavior, it's well to remember that they didn't choose to become selfish and disliked. No one wants to be disliked.

People can also learn to withhold what they have from others because someone has greedily taken it from them before. They may have been the victim of those who were more powerful than them, learning that in order to keep what they have, they have to hide it, clutch onto it tightly, fight, or lie about it, lest they lose it again. Even when they have more than they can use for themselves, they may be stingy, or may never feel like they have enough. This is easily observed with money, but it can also occur with affection, and with time.

The people who are best at giving affection are those who have received it abundantly, and who were praised for giving it in return. They didn't fear losing affection because it was always available. But, if they were deprived of affection or their own affection was rejected, then they would have learned to place other meanings on it. For example, they may have learned that giving affection is something someone "does" in order to get something that he wants (like sex, attention, or money). So, if there is nothing that they are wanting at the moment, they also feel no reason to give affection. This pattern can easily be seen in men who are affectionate only when pursuing women, only when they want to have sex, or only after their relationship is threatened.

A helpful viewpoint for you to have is to see your husband as *unintentionally* depriving himself of having a better relationship with you. He is not intentionally trying to make your life miserable or your relationship worse. His goal is not to make you unhappy. Rather, he is doing his best with limited skills, given his life experience. He wants a good relationship (or least to avoid a bad one), too. He is *not* your enemy. Although helping him to change will make him anxious at first, as he changes, he will enjoy giving as well as getting. Trust and respect will grow between the both of you, and you will both enjoy communicating more. You can't explain this to him. This is something he has to experience before he will be able to understand.

Your interventions will need to give him the opportunity to experience the joy of giving, even though at first he won't want to. He can't learn simply by your telling him about it nor by your complaining about what you don't like. As with other kinds of difficult men, creating new experiences is the key to improving your relationship.

Differentiate Selfishness from Indifference

Selfishness is not the same as indifference. Men who are selfish *seem* not to care, although they actually care very much. Men who are indifferent, on the other hand, *really* don't care. The behavior of these two types of people look the same, but they react differently to the same interventions. A selfish husband is likely to be defensive and angry when you start to make changes. At first he will grumble a lot, but then eventually make a positive adjustment. It's a natural, predictable, and desirable pattern. An indifferent husband, on the other hand, is not likely to be very defensive or angry at all. He is more likely to admit that what he is doing may not be fair, but that it is the way it is. So, if you don't like it, you can lump it. If your husband reacts with indifference, then selfishness is *not* the main problem. The problem is that he is with you for some reason other than a relationship. You will need to work on figuring out his reason for being with you, rather than working on selfishness. Getting professional help for yourself would be a good way for you to deal with a man who is using you for something other than a relationship.

The interventions in this book will work with selfish men because they do care about their relationship. Being put in a position where they may lose the relationship is upsetting for them.

Don't Expect His Cooperation—At First

The first time you deal with your husband's selfish behaviors will be the hardest. He will expect you to behave as you have in the past or like others he has had conflicts with in the past. A strong, but loving approach will be alien to him. The last person who was strong with him may have rejected him. His outward reaction may be either angry or sad, but underneath he will be scared and he won't know what to do. After he discovers that you are neither trying to take something away from him nor rejecting him, he will work with you much more readily. Because your relationship will grow, you will be even more valuable to him. It's important that you remain both strong and loving until you both get to this point.

Looking More Closely at the Intentions Behind Your Husband's Selfishness

Selfishness is an attempt to take care of oneself in a way that just happens to deprive someone else. The goal of selfishness is not to deprive the other person, though. It is rather to take care of oneself. That part of your husband is healthy. We all need to take care of ourselves. Indeed, we have a responsibility to take care of ourselves so that we will be better able to help other people. What he needs to learn is how to get what he wants without depriving you.

When your husband is selfish, what you are probably reacting to most is what you are being deprived of. You are in a position to see that more clearly than he can. He is likely to know that his behavior bothers you, though he may not see it as *depriving* you. If you just forcibly stopped him from doing his selfish behavior (took away his car keys, garnered his wages, refused to have sex, etc.), he would see it as your depriving him—as a hostile act. You would then be depriving him so that he doesn't deprive you—a vicious cycle bound to make your relationship more distant.

Instead of directly trying to block his behavior, it is better to discover the *real motive* of his behavior (that healthy part) and how it helps him or makes him feel good. Then, try to find a way for him to have that without depriving you. Even people who commit crimes or have affairs are motivated by a drive for something good—the need to feel important, the need to connect in a loving way, the need to feel in control, etc. Rarely are people motivated purely by evil. If he is using bill money for his toys, for example, when you do the interventions to change his behavior, also help him to set up a savings account or budget for his toys. If he needs socialization with his friends, make sure that he can continue, but in a way that doesn't deprive you of socialization with him or your friends. Helping each other to get what you both want, but in ways that build the relationship, is a hallmark of a vibrant and growing relationship.

Making Changes: A Three Step Approach

When I work with women who have difficult husbands, unless the behavior is dangerous, I always recommend starting with the softest interventions rather than the most effective ones. Starting with a gentle approach will make more sense to your partner, feel better to you, and will help you to feel more justified in using a stronger approach later, if you need to.

I believe that although partners are responsible for their own behavior, there is some justification in a husband saying, "Why didn't you tell me it bothered you before you filed for divorce?" The first intervention, then, starts with a simple, clear, and positive communication. The second intervention combines communication with the use of a boundary (something you do to prevent a continuation of the current pattern), and the third intervention is one step short of separation or divorce, but with no threats. The third intervention puts your relationship on the line in a positive and controlled way, designed to minimize panic, and promote the relationship. A tough third level intervention is necessary, when divorce or a dead relationship would otherwise occur. It is therefore *only* useful if you predict your relationship will end if his selfish behavior doesn't change. In most cases, level one and level two interventions will be enough.

I recommend that you read through all of the interventions and examples before you try even a level one intervention. As you read the examples, try to imagine how they could be applied to your situation—what you would say and do. Anticipate how your husband would react and how you can effectively prepare for his reactions. Preparing for his reactions will mean that *you* won't become reactive. It's important for your relationship that you be in control, even when he isn't.

Level One Intervention: A Clear and Direct Request

Although you have a very difficult man, communicating with him is your best first step. Even if he refuses to listen to you (the old fingers in the ear and humming routine), he won't be able to honestly say later that you never said anything about it. If anyone does anything that is not good for your relationship, whether it is a friend, relative, or your partner, assume that they don't know what would be better. Amazing as it may seem, not only are many people ignorant of what makes a good relationship, they also have different ideas about what makes a bad one. Many problems can be prevented or solved with clear communication.

A level one intervention is a direct, clear, and positive request, without explanations or debate. It is short and easy to understand. "Please take out the trash every day when you come home," "Please kiss me, caress me, and stimulate me for at least 15 minutes before you have intercourse with me," and "Please take me out once a week," are examples of clear communication. He may disagree or refuse, but he's not likely to misunderstand. For your level one communication, clarity and simplicity is what you are shooting for. If he does what you ask, be sure to thank him and treat him just as you would if he had done it on his own initiative. Don't say, "Thanks for doing what I asked," which emphasizes compliance. Instead, thank him for what he did. "Thanks for taking out the trash—that was very helpful," "The way you stimulated me was great, you did a good job getting me hot," and "Thanks for taking me out," are positive ways to thank your husband. You can include with these expressions whatever non-verbals that would please him.

On the next page you can see a formula for making direct requests as well as three examples. There is nothing wrong with asking your husband for these or other things. Lack of clear and positive communication results in more problems than selfishness does. How many times should you make this request? Twice. More

A Formula for Making a Direct, Clear, and Positive Request

"Please (opposite of what you don't want) (frequency desired)."

	Example 1	Example 2	Example 3
What you don't want	Quickie sex	Use all our spending money for himself	Him to play computer games all the time
Opposite of what you don't want	30 minutes foreplay, one hour sex, I orgasm first	Give me half of the spending money	Shut off the computer one hour before bedtime and be with me
How often you want it	Two times a week	Each pay period	Each night
Request	*"Two times a week, please spend one half an hour doing foreplay with me, then make me orgasm before you do."*	*"Please give me half of the spending money each time you get paid."*	*"Please turn off the computer one hour before bedtime each night and spend that time with me."*

than that is nagging. Fewer than that usually won't be effective, even if he agrees the first time. Make your request. Wait a week, then make it again. If he has not followed through within another week, use a level two intervention.

Level Two Intervention: Refusing and Limit Setting

The refusing I'm referring to here is your refusal to continue to do things in a way which supports your husband's selfishness. Whereas the first level intervention, requesting, depended mainly on his choice to do or not do what you request, the level two intervention takes that choice away from him. You become the one with the choice. You can either choose to continue things as they are, or you can choose to end this negative pattern.

This is actually not a new choice for you. You have had this choice all along, although it may not have been obvious to you. You may have believed that refusing to go along with your husband's selfishness would create serious conflict in your relationship. You may have believed that refusing to go along with what your husband wants would make you the selfish one. You may have even believed that refusing would make your relationship worse. But stopping a bad pattern will in the long run make things better. Allowing destructive patterns to continue is the most harmful choice you could make.

The way you refuse is important. If your method of refusing was to simply say "no," "hell no," "no way," or "sorry, not today," you *could* get an even worse result. Your behavior would be interpreted by your husband as a sort of attack—both on him and on the relationship itself. Of course, you could understand that because you wouldn't want him to simply say "no" to you.

Rather than simply refusing, you must promote the relationship and help your husband to understand the reason for your refusal. It must also allow him to get what he wants, but in a way that isn't selfish.

Let's look at an example of the kind of refusing that I am talking about and then talk about the particulars.

Example Level Two Intervention for a Selfish Husband

Suppose that you have requested (in your level one intervention) that your husband have more foreplay with you before sex and to satisfy your needs as well as his own. But, despite your positive request and desire to please him, he still is orgasm focused (his own) and selfish. For you to continue to go along with this kind of sex would be damaging to you, to your relationship, and ultimately to your husband. You would become less and less positive toward him (especially sexually), less respected by him, and your relationship would suffer. To make things better, you're going to have to refuse to continue things the way they are, but while still making it fairly easy for your husband to change.

Since I don't know your husband's name, I am going to call him "Bob." Here is an approach that you could use with Bob:

You: "Bob, I know that sometimes you like to have sex with me."

Bob: (Grunts, stares, says "I guess so" or possibly picks his teeth).

You: "I have decided that you should have really good sex and get the best from me. You are, after all my husband, and I want us to have a great relationship."

Bob: (Smiles leeringly, checks to see if you are drunk, or says something like, "Well, here it is…")

You: (Ignoring Bob's responses). "That's why I've decided to stop having sex with you the way that we are now. I know you get some satisfaction out of it, but you aren't getting as much of me as you could, and I am becoming more distant from you. I'm really sorry that I have been letting it go on. I don't want to cheat you that way, anymore."

Bob: (Now confused). "What?"

You: "That's right, when I just have sex with you for five minutes and let you go to sleep, I am damaging our relationship. It is making me pull away from you and not be with you. I'm not going to do that to you anymore."

Bob: "Well, I don't mind. It's ok like it is. Don't worry about it."

You: "Bob, you are too important to me to just let it go on like it is. I don't want to lose you."

Bob: *"What are you saying? I can't understand you. You've been watching too much of those women's shows."*

You: *"Well, that may be, but I've decided that I'm only going to have wonderful sex with you. No more quickie sex. I'm not going to contribute to losing this relationship with you."*

Bob: *"What does that mean? I just don't understand what you are saying."*

You: *"What I am saying is that when you want to have sex, we will kiss and touch, and maybe do lots of things, except we won't have intercourse until we have done that for at least 15 minutes. (Start with a small change in the right direction. Demanding that you orgasm first could create extra problems right now)."*

Bob: *"What, should I set a timer?"*

You: *"That might be a good idea. We can call it your 'Go for It' signal."* *(Bob made a suggestion that is not romantic, but it is essentially agreeing with your idea, so, reward it).*

Now, let's look at some of the specific parts of this communication. The first thing you can notice is that Bob is not being asked to agree with anything. Whether he agrees or not does not really matter. Since having sex is under your control, he has no choice. Asking Bob if he agrees invites conflict, since Bob is already satisfied (or else your level one intervention would have worked).

The second thing to notice about this is that Bob is not being blamed for his behavior. Instead, you are taking responsibility for having let it go on. Although he has also been letting it go on, blaming him will only increase his resistance and invite more conflict. Your taking responsibility for letting the behavior go on will be new and confusing for him. It's important that you be sincere and definitely avoid all sarcasm. The fact is (as with this example), you have been letting the behavior go on. This apologetic attitude is always appropriate when you are communicating to your partner that you are no longer going to be codependent (help to maintain a harmful behavior) about something. In this example, it is quickie, one-way sex. Other examples, could be misspending money, adultery, drug or alcohol addictions, and many others. Usually for a relationship to continue with one partner doing these behaviors, the other partner has to be codependent in some way. Change starts to happen when the codependency stops. Stopping it for the sake of your relationship expresses love and the desire for a better relationship. Your partner can still react angrily, but a rejected partner is harder to deal with, in the long run, than a partner who is temporarily angry because he needs to change his behavior.

A third thing to notice about this intervention is that there is some benefit in it for Bob. He is to get "great sex" instead of his usual sex. His desire for sexual release is not bad, even though his behavior is selfish. People don't do things just to be bad. An alcoholic may want to deal with stress, or connect socially with his drinking buddies. A gambler may want to feel excitement or to hit it big. Helping your husband to change means helping him to have even more of what he wants, but in a way that promotes the relationship. That is what being a good partner is all about. Without concern for what he needs or wants, you would just be perceived as the "relationship police." Many men become secretive for fear of losing what is important to them should their wife find out. Generally, they will change their behavior if you can help them to appropriately get what it is that is motivating their inappropriate behavior. But of course the inappropriate behavior must stop.

One final note about this intervention. If the eventual change he needs to make is a big one, start with a small change, as with the above example (15 minutes of foreplay). Perhaps what you really want is a romantic evening, a half-hour of foreplay, your own orgasm, and then his five minute release. Such big changes occur more easily after successful small changes. Requiring such a large change all at once would appear selfish (Bob would see it as "having to" give 3 hours to you just so he can have 5 minutes of sex). With such perceived inequality, he could grow resentful and choose to give up sex or get it elsewhere, which would cause even more harm to your relationship.

I have spoken about our example man, Bob, in rather harsh terms. Most men are considerably more reasonable. But, if you know how to deal with the worst of men, it is much easier to deal with men who aren't as bad. I want to teach you how to handle the most difficult situations so that you can feel confident, so that you can feel right, and so that you can have success, for your sake as well as your husband's.

This intervention of refusal, which is a level two intervention, doesn't always work. Some men would rather work around you than with you—even if makes their life more difficult to do so. If a month has gone by without improvement, *and if continuing without change risks your relationship*, then a level three intervention will be necessary.

Level Three Intervention: Individuating without Separation

Because of the seriousness of your relationship problems and because less intense interventions have not been successful, this intervention is only one step ahead of separation. It definitely should not be used before thoroughly trying both level one (requesting) and level two (refusing) interventions. When you have used both level one and level two interventions with your husband, this level three intervention will be understandable for him, although he won't like it. If you suddenly used this more severe intervention without first using gentle and moderate interventions, your actions would make you appear like you were overreactive, no matter how right you were. Your husband can't see what you think—he can only hear what you say and only see what you do. Although something may have been bothering you for a long time, that needs to first be communicated to him in a gentle way, then boundaries need to be set in a firm way, and then lastly a very tough way. With such a graduated approach, usually over a period of a few months (except for bombshell issues like affairs), he has time to think, make changes, adjust, and become fully informed of the damage that is happening in the relationship. By the time you do a level three intervention, he will have no excuses for not knowing what you want or what he needs to do for the relationship to be better.

At level three, he is going to get the message that change is urgently needed because the relationship is in danger. While a man can get this message by being told by his wife that she wants a divorce, the "D" word is rejecting, often causes a panic, followed by a short term change in behavior, followed by a return to previous behavior once the danger of divorce is past. Also, when a woman gets to the point where she tells her husband that she is wanting to divorce him, something changes inside her. An emotional gap can be created that can be hard to close—particularly if her partner doesn't know how to help her to be close again. Men who are faced with divorce rarely know how to win back their wife's love. For those reasons, I don't consider threatening divorce to be a good intervention to create change. It's like trying to fix a computer with a hammer.

At level three, you have already talked clearly and positively to your husband about what you want, you have also refused to be codependent for his selfish behaviors. Now, you are going to take him out of the loop. He is going to start to feel like things are slipping out of control. He needs to be a little shaken up. Although that will inevitably lead to some conflict, the conflict can be managed—continuing to live with his selfishness cannot. In other words, at this point, you should have decided that doing nothing will lead to the end of your relationship. If you can't say that, then his behavior *is* acceptable to you, although you don't like it. If that is the case, then don't do this intervention.

At level three, your intervention is an effort to save a relationship that would otherwise crash and burn. You will be like the pilot who has to tell people to get into crash position. It is bound to raise feelings of panic and desperation, but still with some hope. As bad as this situation seems, it is infinitely better than the pilot donning a parachute and jumping out the door, leaving the passengers no hope of a safe landing. It takes tough love to do tough interventions in a relationship. It requires only self-love to cut and run. This intervention is as much a measure of your love and your commitment to the relationship as it is of your husband's love and commitment to you.

Again, as with the second level intervention, I am going to give you an example first, and then talk about the various parts of this intervention.

Example Preliminary Talk with a Sexually Selfish Husband (optional)

(The preliminary talk is optional as I will discuss after the example).

You: *"Bob, I have been really unsuccessful at improving this relationship in some very important areas. Because of this, we are both getting to the point where our relationship may need to end. We are not there yet, and I am going to do what I can to save our relationship."*

Bob: *"I'm tired of your nagging, etc., etc."*

You: *"You're right, Bob, the things I have done have really not been helpful in improving our relationship... I need to do something different if our relationship is to survive. I don't want to lose you."*

Bob: *"What the hell does that mean?!"*

You: *"It means this is my last chance to make things better for us."*

Bob: *"? I don't get it."*

You: *"I know Bob. I'm sorry."*

Bob: *"(bewildered and confused). Whatever."*

This is an optional talk that precedes the actual intervention. The intervention can be done without this talk, but I'm a believer in being open and honest and sending a clear message that what you are doing is for the sake of the relationship. I also believe that it is more effective to tell men things twice. This talk, though, will accomplish nothing except to lose you respect if you don't follow through with the intervention. So, if you are in doubt about following through, it's better to say nothing first. You can save this talk until after the stuff hits the fan, if you prefer.

This preliminary talk, just as with the second level intervention, does not blame your husband for his behavior, but rather has you take responsibility for not effectively changing things. Unless your husband is among the most difficult of men, he will also confess to having made things difficult. But, don't hold out for that nor try to get him to say that. Don't argue with him if he does or doesn't admit to something, and don't try to force an admission from him. Instead, honestly take responsibility for not doing something more effective (as you are going to do). It may not seem fair, but it's more important to change things at this point than to seek fairness.

Example Level Three Intervention for a Sexually Selfish Husband

You: "Bob I'm very concerned about our relationship."

Bob: "(sarcastically) So, what else is new?"

You: "(ignoring Bob's comment) my request for you to satisfy me sexually wasn't helpful. And my attempt to set conditions on the way we have sex wasn't helpful either."

Bob: "I suppose you think it's my fault."

You: "No, I tried something that didn't work. Sex is an important part of our relationship for me. And I need to know whether this is going to continue, so I can plan well for my future."

Bob: "What do you mean?"

You: "I mean that if I can't have good sex with you, then we would need to end the relationship. It's not what I want, but I'm not willing to live in a sexless marriage."

Bob: "Well, you're to blame..."

you: "I may be to blame. But I won't live in a sexless marriage, so whether we continue is up to you."

Bob: "Well, then we continue."

You: "I'm glad you want to. I do too, if things change. But, if they don't change within 30 days, your decision will be clear."

Bob: "Thirty days?"

You: "Yes. I'm going to mark it on the calendar."

Bob: "What are you going to do in 30 days?"

You: "By then I will know whether you have decided this is going to be a sexless marriage. It will also give you a chance to come up with an even better solution for us. I can't keep you from having a sexless relationship if that is what you prefer, but I won't be a part of it."

Bob: "So, you are threatening me?"

You: "No. I'm giving you the choice of whether you want a sexless marriage or one with me. One more thing, Bob. If you wait to see what I will do, I'm not sure I will be able to recover from the hurt, even if you change."

Notice in this level three intervention that you continue not to blame Bob. If you did, it would lead to conflict, which is counterproductive. You can't get to a closer relationship through conflict. Instead you continue to take responsibility for not having effectively dealt with the situation (which is true). You show your resolve to do something effective or to lose the relationship, because it's that important to you.

Although Bob can blame you, he can't say this isn't an important issue for you. So allow him to blame you if he wants, but don't be sidetracked by that. Instead, state your desire to save the relationship, but your unwillingness to keep the relationship as it is (*this must be true for this intervention to work*).

Thirty days notice is plenty of time for him to decide if it's worth giving you sexual satisfaction (in this example), in order to keep the relationship. Although this may seem like you are threatening to divorce unless he changes, the dynamics are very different. You are giving him time to decide how important the relationship is to him. You are giving him time to decide whether he cares about what you want. It's the visible result of these decisions which will let you know whether he cares about you or not. Threatening to divorce would be a one-sided power play. This intervention is actually a shared decision, with your stated desire to have a good relationship with your husband. He also knows that what you really want is to have a good sexual relationship with him. He isn't rejected—only the way you are both living is. It is important to give Bob choices. He can change or not, and he can also think of other solutions. Who knows, maybe he will come up with a good idea or at least ideas worth trying.

Intervention for Non-Sexual Issues

With other than sexual issues, you can work around your husband—make up for his selfishness instead of waiting for him to do it. If you are resenting your husband for not helping around your home, don't just let it become messy. Hire someone to help. If you can't afford to do that, get your own bank account and cut money out of the budget or get a job to be able to fund it, decrease expenses in other areas, sell things on eBay, or have a lawn sale. Or you can take time away from other things you usually do for your husband. The idea is to stop waiting for generosity from a selfish man. If you're thinking you shouldn't have to make any changes, remind yourself this is temporary. It's an intervention. It's not a new way of life.

If your husband won't spend any time with you or take you out, go out without him. With your friends. If you don't have friends, then make some. Get a hobby, join a club. But don't wait around for him to take you out. In essence, you are working to become independent of your husband in areas where he is most selfish. At some time you both will reach a point where you are satisfied with the changes you have made, or where he blows up. Either of these two are preferable to your being a martyr, by doing nothing but be patient, which is sure to kill your relationship. Never be afraid of your husband getting upset, or he will get upset more and more. Learn how to respond to upset people if you don't know how (see the chapter on the angry man). It's a great skill to have.

Sometimes when women become more independent, they are surprised to find that although their husbands grumble a little, they basically agree with the change. They pay for the housekeeper or child care, they watch the kids so their wives can go out, they support her having her own expense account, etc. In other words, some men respond to this simply as they would to reasonable assertiveness. You may end up wishing that you did these things years ago rather than trying to get him to go along with the program.

Other men, more difficult, will more than likely become upset and confront you about decisions you made "without them," "behind their backs," and "against the relationship." This upset, is actually a sign of progress. Your husband wouldn't be upset if he didn't care. You have finally got his attention in a way that your words did not before. Now is not the time to fight, though. It is the time to give him a choice.

He will ask you why you did or are doing such things. Even though you may have told him before, he didn't understand at that time, didn't listen well, or doesn't remember. Which it is doesn't make any difference. Now, he is beginning to understand that something needs to change, and he needs to be told again, clearly.

Example Level Three Intervention for Non-Sexual Issues

Bob: "Are you crazy?! We can't afford this (or any other message that your behavior is terrible)."

You: "It was either that or divorce you. But, I don't want to lose you, so I was trying to save our marriage."

Bob: "What are you saying?"

You: "I'm just trying to save our marriage. I know that you don't want to give me the help I need to stay in the marriage, so I was trying to find some other way. But, if you don't want me to use any other way to be happy either, then I guess we will just need to let our relationship come to an end. I am so sorry. I was doing my best to save our relationship."

Bob: "(*shocked*) *You mean to tell me that if you don't have a maid (go out with your friends, have your own spending money, etc.) that you are going to divorce me?*"

You: "*I can see clearly that without your help and with no other way to do things, our relationship is going to die. I don't want it to, but I know you can see it too.*"

Bob: "*Things would be ok if you weren't so...*"

You: "*That may be true, but I am what I am. I can give you 30 days more to be sure of how much you want to keep this relationship. But if things aren't going to change, I don't want to continue our relationship like this.*"

Because you are not fighting Bob, the conflict can't escalate. You continue not to blame him. You continue to say how important your relationship is to you. You even agree with him if he blames you. If Bob cares about the relationship, he may storm off or shut down. Either one means that he needs to think about it by himself. Be sure you make no attempt to follow him or open him up. Bob will, in time, either decide to help you, will come up with another idea, or will agree that you two should get a divorce. He will only agree with the divorce if he doesn't want to continue your relationship. Since you have decided that your marriage cannot continue without change, at this point you both would be in agreement that it's better to end things than to continue as you are. This is serious stuff for a serious problem. You need to be taken seriously, so that your relationship has a chance—a chance that it would not have otherwise.

I don't teach you this method because I want you to get a divorce. I teach you this method so that you won't have to. Unless you can accept his behavior, or unless you do an intervention, your relationship will deteriorate to the divorce point. This intervention provides a healthy opportunity for change by creating a crisis, then offering your husband a way to resolve the crisis and save the marriage. Without precipitating the crisis early, it would eventually come by itself, but after you are both too burned out to care.

As you can see, this intervention involves communication skills and problem solving skills. If you like, you can get a few *coaching* sessions on the skills and increase your effectiveness. Most *counselors* support divorce or divorce threats when a level two intervention doesn't work. I wanted to show you, though, that it is possible to be extremely tough (a level three intervention) without ever rejecting your husband. I believe that once a partner rejects another, there is deep damage done to the relationship which is never really forgotten. The level three intervention gets through to the selfish man without rejecting him. It gives him an opportunity to change and it paints a clear picture of what is going to happen if he doesn't. And, because there is no blaming on your part, conflict is minimal.

Typically a level three intervention is not required. Usually, when I help a woman to do a good level two intervention, it is enough. When you can be sure that each step you take is a good one, it's not emotionally difficult to move on to the next one.

Dealing with the Financially Selfish Husband

A financially selfish husband takes money away from the needs of his family (even if it is just the two of you) to pay for non-essential expenses. He may also use any extra money that you both have to enjoy himself, no matter how miserable you are. This is not a situation you will want to allow to continue. You can start to improve this situation by starting with a level one intervention, clearly requesting the behavior you want, as in the following examples.

Example Level One Interventions for a Financially Selfish Husband

"Please make a budget with me so we can pay our bills and both have spending money."

"Please give me your paycheck so I can pay the bills first and so we can get out of debt."

Your request should be clear and specific. If he wants information so he can understand better, then be ready to show him on paper the financial situation. Remember that your request does not blame. It solves. If he refuses, don't argue. Arguing won't help, but a level two intervention will.

Be sure to give him some time to respond to the level one intervention (at least a week, but no more than four), and make sure you do it two times (but not more than that). Then, if necessary, continue with a level two intervention.

Example Level Two Intervention: for a Financially Selfish Husband

You: "Bob, I need to apologize to you. I've been letting something go on that's damaging our relationship. You are too important to me to let it get to the point where our relationship needs to end."

Bob: "What are you talking about?"

You: "I've just been standing aside while you use money for your hobbies that we need for bills (or without me having any money of my own to enjoy). Although I know it is working for you, it is making our relationship more distant."

Bob: "Well, maybe you better realize that it's my money. I earn it, or at least most of it."

You: "Yes, you can have the money Bob. I need time to make my own money, though, so I'm turning over shopping and childcare to you."

Bob: "That's extreme. I'm not going to do that, that's your job."

You: "Well, I could do it, but I don't want to do my job if you're the only one who gets paid for doing it. No, that would kill our relationship for sure. Already you can feel how distant we are becoming."

As with the other communications, take responsibility for *solving* the problem. What you do should be logically connected to what he does. If he uses too much money, you either need to cut somewhere or make more.

Don't blame your husband for creating the problem (even though he did). Make a clear statement about your desire to be close to him and to not lose the relationship. Men who care, often don't respond to the "wanting to be close" message, but they don't want to lose their wives. And never threaten to divorce. Just point out what is obvious—the increasing distance and the likelihood of the relationship ending if something doesn't change. The extra burden of managing more by himself (such as shopping, and so on) will help him to understand, on an *emotional* level, the seriousness of the situation. Of course you can use other problem-solving methods (e.g. sell personal stuff that belongs to you and Bob, start your own business, hire a consultant, etc.). The important thing is not to carry on with business as usual. He will never believe the relationship is in danger if you are willing to carry on without it changing. If you think the idea of him doing childcare is extreme (given his job, for example), consider the childcare he would need to do for child visitations after you divorce. It may be a very important piece of reality that he needs right now.

Example Level Three Intervention for a Financially Selfish Man

If level one and level two interventions didn't work, and if your relationship won't last unless changes are made, it is time for a level three intervention. Your only other choices would be to continue on as you are until the relationship dies, or divorce. At level three, he needs to clearly feel the relationship slipping away.

You: "Bob, I'm very concerned about our relationship."

Bob: "*(sarcastically) So, what else is new?*"

You: "*(ignoring Bob's comment) my request for you to help me financially wasn't helpful. And my attempt to improve my financial situation wasn't very helpful either.*"

Bob: "*Well, I told you it was a stupid plan.*"

You: "*I can see you were right. Feeling like things are fair is important to me, and I need to know if we are just going to continue this way, so I can plan for my future.*"

Bob: "*What do you mean?*"

You: "*I mean that our marriage won't last this way. We will just become more and more distant. I don't want that to happen, but you can see that it will if we keep going this way.*"

Bob: "*Well, you're to blame...*"

You: "*I may be to blame. But I can't be happy in a relationship that I feel is so unfair.*"

Bob: "*Your feelings are messed up. Other women would be satisfied.*"

You: "*Probably many women would be satisfied. But now I know that you are the only one who can save this relationship. I can't just keep waiting. I think 30 days will give me enough time to see how our relationship is going to go.*"

Bob: "*Thirty days?*"

You: "*Yes, I will mark it on the calendar.*"

Bob: "*What happens in 30 days?*"

You: "*I will know by then whether things are going to change or whether I need to plan for a future without you. It's not what I want and I'm not going to do it now, but then I will need to.*"

Bob: "*Are you threatening me?*"

You: "*No way. I just want to deal with reality. You are free to choose how you want things to be. But I know I can't continue like this. Life is too short.*"

Bob: "*Whatever.*"

As with the other level three interventions, there is no arguing, and no blaming (on your part). There is an expressed desire to have a better relationship with your husband and a clear message that you won't continue as you are. Bob is not controlled by your words—he is given control over whether the relationship continues or not. You are sharing the decision. There is nothing that he needs to agree with. Nothing to argue about. So whether he agrees or not, don't argue.

Dealing With the Man Who Won't Help Out at Home (or Any Situation Which is Really Unfair)

Before doing this intervention, help yourself to be convinced of whether he is being selfish or not by making a list of how you both spend your time. Then, see if you can decrease what you do in a way that makes things more comfortable for the both of you. Some women are doing far more at home than their husbands expect, because they have too high of an expectation for what should be done. If you can slack up without your husband making any demands on you, then you may be trying to live up to your own unrealistic expectations, with the result that you feel overworked and drained, as well as irritated when your husband plops down in front of the TV. It may be well to talk with your husband about his expectations regarding what you are doing before deciding that he is doing too little. You may be doing too much.

Assuming that you are doing a lot more of what really needs to be done, with little or no help from your husband, who just treats you like a servant, or worse—like his doting mother, it is time to take action. Applying a level one intervention, you would make a direct, clear, and positive request—perhaps with a little organizational help thrown in. For example:

Example Level One Intervention for an Unfair Man

You: "Bob, when you come home each day, please check this board (a whiteboard in the kitchen) for what your jobs are. My jobs will be listed, too. We can do what needs to be done then do what we want in a more relaxed way. It would really help."

Bob: "Ok."

Now, since you are reading this book, it's not going to be as easy as that, is it? Still, it's the place to start. Always do a level one intervention before a level two intervention, which comes before a level three intervention. Let's see what the level two intervention would look like.

Example Level Two Intervention for an Unfair Man

You: "Bob, I've realized that I've been making myself resent you. I've been doing far too much, even when I didn't have to. As a result, I've been becoming more and more resentful toward you. That's making us more distant. I am sorry. I've decided it's better to let some things go undone rather than become more distant from you. Our relationship is more important to me than getting things done at home, and I don't want to lose it."

Bob: "Well, I always told you to relax more. You should take it easy like I do."

You: "Yes, you are right. So, I've decided to give up cooking dinner and ironing your clothes. Instead, I will just focus on the things that are really important for keeping a nice home."

Bob: "But, I'm your husband. It's your job to cook for me and iron my clothes. You have to do it."

You: "I used to think so too. But, I've decided our relationship is more important and if I just keep going like I have been, our relationship will be dead. Done. Then, you would have to do your own cooking and ironing anyway. Plus, we would have no relationship."

Notice that with this level two intervention, you are not blaming Bob for not helping, you are not reminding him how you have asked him to help time and time again, you are not asking for his agreement, and you are not offering solutions (such as buying something to eat on the way home from work). You are instead taking responsibility for having maintained the situation which is causing the resentment (which is true), and for changing the situation. Bob certainly isn't going to volunteer to change the situation.

After some grumbling and time in his emotional cave, Bob may decide that it's better to help you out some than let you make changes. He may not actually do anything until *after* he sees you make changes and maintain them. So, don't give up when you don't see him change right away! Also, remember—there is no need to be angry with this intervention. In fact, it's counterproductive. It's much better to be both loving and sincere. Don't cook dinner or iron, but do be extra loving. Let him know how much the extra time is making you feel close to him. Thank him.

Suppose that your husband is unmoved even after a month or two of your level two intervention and he is still being far too selfish for your relationship to continue long-term. You will either have to do a level three intervention, fight, or continue to patiently maintain the bad situation—waiting for things to magically get better. *If* you believe that doing nothing would lead to the end of your relationship, the level three intervention will be the best choice. You are not risking much with a strong intervention if your relationship would end anyway.

Example Level Three Intervention for an Unfair Man

You: *"Bob, I have to admit—I'm not doing very well at making things fair enough for our relationship to withstand the strain. I know if I don't make some changes, our relationship is going to end. I think you can sense it too. We are becoming more and more distant and there are no signs of it getting better."*

Bob: *"It's your fault, I'm a wonderful man and do everything to make you happy."*

You: "Yes Bob, I really appreciate everything you do. I can see you are satisfied with things the way they are. It's me who isn't. Maybe I should be, but that's the way it is. Something either has to change or we will surely lose our relationship. I don't want that to happen."

Bob: "Well, I don't either."

You: "Then, let's give this 30 more days to change. By then we will know for sure if we need to end our relationship."

Bob: "Thirty days?"

You: "Yes, I will mark it on the calendar. I hope things can change because I don't want to lose you. But I need to deal with reality. So if things don't change, I will plan for a future without you. Life is too short for waiting and hoping."

By refusing to argue, and because of your previous level two intervention, your point about the relationship should hit home. Again, you are not threatening to divorce Bob. You are merely pointing out the truth which he may be closing his eyes to—that you both are becoming more distant and there will come a point when you won't want to be together anymore. You emphasize that you don't want that. You give Bob time to digest this and decide what is really important to him. Any man who really cares about his relationship will start problem solving.

Troubleshooting the Interventions

Problem #1: <u>Your husband disagrees with what you are saying</u>. No troubleshooting is required, since he is not required to agree. There is nothing to agree with or argue about. You simply decide, communicate, and do. Don't argue, no matter how upset he is. Arguing does not cure someone from being upset. Just let him be upset while you follow through. He will adjust, you will earn respect, and change will happen.

Problem #2: <u>Your husband changes temporarily and then returns to his old selfish ways</u>. This is to be expected. Think of it as a kind of "testing" your resolve. You pass this test by following through as you did before.

Problem #3: <u>Your husband says he will change, but then doesn't.</u> He has attempted to use words to satisfy you. Some women fall for this all the time. You can safely ignore his words and focus on his behaviors. If he promises you the moon, don't believe it until you are holding a piece of moon rock.

You Will Soon Become the Special Irreplaceable Woman in His Life

When you are doing the interventions to change your selfish husband, you may be tempted to think of yourself as selfish— needing him to change so that you can be happy. If that were the only truth in this situation, I might be tempted to agree with you. But, the other truth is that helping him to not be selfish will improve his relationship with you and help him to get more of what he is really after in the first place—more happiness, more self contentment, and a more meaningful life. That's why he committed to you in the first place.

Because he will end up with a better situation than he would if you did nothing, you are *helping* him. You are not being selfish. You are giving him a new level of relationship currently blocked by his insecurities. Selfish people are insecure people. But by your being the strong one, he can do what he could not do on his own— become more secure, make healthy changes, and get even more out of his relationship with you.

In essence, the real test of your relationship is how much your husband is willing to change to keep you. But, when you are able to do interventions that help him, rather than reject him, you lend to him your strength.

Women who threaten divorce or who separate as an intervention may find that their husbands really do care, but are still unable to change on their own. This is true even if the man gets counseling. Without his wife's support, failure is likely. A man, in the midst of changing, benefits greatly from a woman who supports those changes by being strong when she has to (by setting good boundaries), and by being gentle whenever she can. This tough but loving approach is characteristic of close relationships, including husband and wife, parent and child, and close friends. It is a central tenet in all my coaching.

Ongoing Selfishness Should Be Nipped in the Bud

Successfully dealing with your husband's selfish behavior means that he is never going to do anything selfish again, right? Don't count on it. Old habits die hard. If you again start to feel resentful about your husband's behavior, don't wait until things get bad to do a level one intervention. This will make things easier for both of you. If there is something your husband is wanting or needing, find out what it is, and help him to get it in a way that is good for both of you. This avoids selfishness issues. After all, it's not selfish to stop him from doing something if you are helping him to get the object of that behavior in a better way. Just working together like that will do a lot to promote your relationship. "What are you doing?" "What are you trying to accomplish?" and, "How can I help you to get it in a way that is good for both of us?" are internal questions for you to develop about your husband's behavior. Stop any habit you have of asking, "Why is he doing such and such to me?" Instead, ask why he is doing such and such for himself. The answer will be more revealing and closer to the truth. It's not about you, it's about him. As trust and communication grow, you will be able to ask more directly what he wants, work together, and grow closer. Cooperation builds closeness.

If All Else Fails (and Even if It Doesn't)

Do these interventions ever fail? Sure they do. Some husbands don't recognize the value of what they have until it is gone. With the graduated interventions you give them a good chance to decide before it is too late, and in a way in which you can work together. Even so, things don't always go as you wish.

If the interventions don't work, there may be something extra tough about your situation that you haven't noticed, which is preventing success. If so, working with a professional, such as a relationship coach, can help you to uncover the missing piece needed for success. There is never a reason to just be patient with a behavior which is destroying your relationship.

You can learn more about marriage coaching at **coachjackito.com**.

Section Three: Making Love Last

"Love is friendship that has caught fire. It is quiet understanding, mutual confidence, sharing and forgiving. It is loyalty through good and bad times. It settles for less than perfection and makes allowances for human weaknesses."
Ann Landers

11

BEYOND PROBLEMS, CREATING LASTING INTIMACY

This book was written to help you not just with the obstacle that your husband is presenting right now (his negative, habit based behaviors), but also with the wonderful relationship that can follow. Making a win-win plan is much easier, once this obstacle of difficult behavior is out of the way. There will be a temptation, of course, just to enjoy the fruits of your labors, getting along without difficulty. It really is so nice just to be without this obstacle, compared to how it used to be. It is like a whole new start on your relationship. And that is exactly what it is— a new start. Like learning the alphabet. Now, it is time to grow from here.

Each day of your relationship, each day of your life, is a new start on all that will follow. There is no need to go backwards or to spend much time thinking about the past when things are going well in the present. The happy memories, of course, you will never lose and can share at the quiet moments. But just sharing memories is for people too old to make any more. And that's not you, is it? I hope no matter what your age, you are not too old to make new memories of wonderful times. Life doesn't stop until we stop living it.

The end product of your interventions with your husband, as laid out in this book, is not just your husband interacting more nicely with you. Rather, it's both of you enjoying being with each other more. The way you are learning to help your husband also creates an opportunity to work together on a future you might otherwise not have had. In order to share much, you need to be at the point where there is trust, so open sharing does not come until after your initial interventions, and after you trust each other. Even then sharing doesn't happen all at once. It starts small and builds gradually until you are sharing dreams. Everyone has a dream, whether it is a little girl dreaming of getting an ice cream cone or a pensioner dreaming of winning the lottery.

The Problem Behind Low Intimacy is Not What You Think It Is

Is your husband's behavior the problem behind low intimacy? Not really. Admittedly, most women would say that it is because it prevents intimacy. And, many coaches and counselors would agree with them, declaring the relationship problem to be solved when their husband changes. If this really were *the* problem, then such a change should lead to a continuous and happy relationship. And yet, most of the time it does not. It takes more than a lack of problems to create intimacy and happiness.

I have watched numerous couples go through the process of counseling, coaching, and attending marriage retreats and emerge believing that they would then be close once and for all. For the moment, it did seem that way. They were, after all, enjoying each other again, sometimes for the first time in years. They felt positive and hopeful. Some healing had definitely taken place. Part of their feeling close at that time did come from solving problems, but most of it was actually the result of working together, helping each other, on a common goal. For intimacy to continue, such working together needs to continue, even when there are no more problems.

When I was working as a marriage and family counselor, like most counselors, I believed the major focus of all treatment was to return people to their "previously good level of functioning" as the psychology jargon goes. But, most of the time, the improvement in the relationship did not last. Within 6 months to one year, the relationship would begin to slide backward. Six months to one year after that, relationships were often at an all-time low.

What had happened, or not happened, to make things bad again? Something important had not been addressed in their counseling work, something that would ensure not only the end of conflict, but continuing growth as well. Although couples had learned to work on their problems, becoming good problem solvers, they did not learn how to grow when there were no problems. Without growth, even the best of situations can become stale. When that happens, it's easy for old problems to return. When old problems do return, they are experienced differently than before. They bring more sadness, more tiredness, and more hopelessness. Relationships need more than a lack of problems to be enjoyed.

The reason lasting change does not occur for many couples in counseling is that they work on overcoming their relationship problems, but are left on their own to create a generative, meaningful, and growing relationship. And many people simply don't know how to do that. For couples who are already in the process of raising a family or running a business (both being generative and requiring cooperation), nothing more is needed. Counseling has done its job. But for many modern couples, there is no cooperative venture, no real need for each other beyond the emotional. These couples are at a loss as to how to help each other and instead expect romance to do all the work of maintaining their relationship. A relationship can't survive on romance any more than we can survive on candy. Romance-only relationships are better suited to singles, but even so they will still be missing out on the deeper benefits of marriage.

Although there are practical reasons to marry, most couples marry because they believe it to be better than staying single; to be happier, and to share their life. When we marry, we gain a partner who can help us feel what we could not feel by ourselves, can help us do what we could not do by ourselves, and who wants to share in our success as well as our sorrows. We don't marry to compromise and get the most we can while giving the least in return. Compromising is what we do when we buy or rent a home (we want to live in a better house, but we can't afford to), what we do when we accept our jobs (we want higher pay, or a different career, but take what we can get) and what we always do with a world full of people who mainly care about what *they* want. But in marriage, there is no need for compromise of this kind. Marriage is an additive process, not a subtractive one.

A man and woman can uncompromisingly help each other to get everything they want, to be whatever they want to be, and to do whatever they want to do. Although marriage brings responsibility, it gives us more freedom than before because we have more help than before. I have told my wife, "I will help you to get everything you want, so dream big." She now has the freedom to do many things she couldn't do when she was single because she has my help and support. When couples have this kind of attitude, they become very valuable to each other, feel deeply in love, and protect their relationship. No one wants to lose someone valuable. And no person is as valuable as someone who helps you to have the kind of life you want. Someone who is ready to say "yes," rather than "no," is not a person you are ever going to want to leave.

This kind of vision and excitement and forward moving action is what is missing from many troubled relationships. Husbands and wives don't have to have the same dreams to work together and help each other. When people are free to dream, they love their life. When they feel put in a box, on a shelf, like their dreams are unimportant, or like they have to give up their dreams, the relationship is drained of energy. An insecure partner is like a backpack full of stones that we carry around every day. We can only keep an emotional charge, based on happy memories, for so long before we need something new.

Once problems have been solved and a boost given to the relationship, couples need to know specifically how to keep moving forward. Where we are going needs to be more enticing than where we have been. No matter your financial level, you and your husband can learn to do that.

The "Partnership" Model

Following a *therapeutic* model, problems are solved once "symptoms" are gone. In the process many couples become problem solvers (a great skill), but even problem-less, they are not able to work productively on a relationship that they really want to have. They've practiced and become good at romance, become proficient at paying bills and budgeting, learned to communicate about problems big and small, and learned to enjoy dating each other. But they haven't learned how to be "partners." Though they both have a vague idea of what they want from life, they continue to struggle as individuals to achieve it. They lack a feeling of oneness that partnering brings. It's true that every couple has to first learn to get along and remove baggage and barriers. These are as essential to relating as learning the alphabet is to reading and writing. After that, comes putting the skills together, not to work on solving problems, but to work on the future. With the *partnering* model, the more they work as partners, the closer they will be.

The Two Prerequisites to Partnership

There can be no partnership of any kind without: 1) respect, and 2) trust. You can work on getting these with skills like the ones in this book. Once you can really trust each other, sharing will go smoothly. Couples who can share dreams and plans can have the excitement of making those plans and dreams come true. Like a cake without frosting, many couples are missing out on the biggest benefit marriage brings—being one in mind, one in heart, and one in *purpose*. Respect, trust, and sharing makes that possible. Sharing good times and good memories can be joyful; sharing the future can be motivating and exciting.

Partnering Starts with Dreams and Desires

To achieve any goal, including having a good relationship, it is important to start with the end in mind. Just as Michelangelo carved the marble statue of David, chip by chip, we also must work from the beginning. The start of our work is to have a clear idea of what we want to create. Otherwise, we will just end up with a pile of marble chips and no statue. When we cook, create, make, or build something, we need to know what we are making. Otherwise, what we make usually turns out to be a mess. Without plans, we will end up asking ourselves after years have slipped by, "Where did my life go?" "What happened to that relationship that I wanted to have?" and finally, "I can't believe I wasted my life on unimportant things, and now it is too late." Getting specific about what we want moves us forward and helps us to enjoy the process. Regrets are preventable if we can realize early on to live life forward. Our windshield of life needs to be bigger than our rearview mirror.

What helps to move us from thinking to action is getting *specific* about what we want. Vague ideas won't lead to action or partnership. It is no more specific to say that you want to have a good relationship than it is to say that you want to have a good career or a good sandwich. Nor is it specific to say you want to communicate well and enjoy each other's company. Or have a happy life. You know your ideas are too vague when they don't translate into action. On the other hand, "I want to be a waiter at a five-star restaurant (corporate lawyer, English teacher, finish carpenter, etc.)" is more specific. It is more motivating, and more action-producing than saying "I want to have a good career." When we get specific, we know what our next steps are or can easily find out. We can clearly *imagine* it. And we can only do what we can imagine. Having a "good career," is like sailing in a fog to reach a mystical island. To actually have a good career, you must first decide what kind of career you want to have. "A good one" says only that you don't want to have a bad one. It doesn't tell you where to start, where to go, or what your future is likely to be like. In the same way, although your partner may agree with you about having a "good relationship," his image of that may be very different from yours. Getting specific, together, will allow for action and partnering to begin. It will give you a lot to talk about. This may be something you have never done with anyone, but something that is now possible with your husband once the trust is in place.

In couple's coaching we get moving by starting with specifics and you can do the same. To do this, use a piece of paper and pencil, or keyboard these things right now. First, list everything you want to achieve, accomplish, have, and be in your life. It's important to get out all of those desires that are inside you. Just make a list of big things, small things, silly things, serious things—anything you like. It makes no difference if they are achievable or not, moral or not, affordable or not. You're not committed to doing any of these things. Trying to censor your list will block too many good ideas. Making a list of 100 things would be a good start, but even 50 would be ok. Our inner dreams are the measuring stick for our current satisfaction with life. The more different they are from our reality, the less satisfied we are. Dreams, hopes, and desires are also a large part of what explain differences in people's feelings. How other people relate to our dreams and desires accounts for many of the feelings we have toward them. Necessarily, many of the things we have secretly wanted remain hidden and we dare not show them to others. Amazingly, happily, within a trusting and secure relationship, our dreams can be shared. When they are shared and accepted, the bond between two people becomes very tight. Our understanding grows deeper. (By the way, if it was hard to list 100 things, I will just tell you "of course" like I do for my clients. Nothing good ever comes easily). I recommend you finish your list before moving on to the next paragraph.

After listing desires, organizing them comes next. What are the big desires? The little ones? The medium ones? Which ones will need to happen before the other ones can happen? Which ones do you *have to* have? Which ones are ok to lose? How could your partner begin to help you to realize them? How can you help your partner to achieve his dreams? When couples start thinking like this, they become very enthusiastic about working together. The more you can organize and prioritize your goals, the easier it will be to achieve them.

Involving Your Husband in This Process

"Honey, let's talk" is not very motivating to most men once they have been married for awhile. For him, talking usually feels like something he *has* to do because it is part of his *job* as a husband. "Honey, let's talk about how I can help you to get everything you want," is a whole lot more appealing. Men become eager to help their wives get what they want when their wives help them get what they want (this is not compromise because no one is giving up anything). There is nothing wrong on working on getting what you want. Actually, there is something very right about it. All successful people do that. All of the religious leaders have done that. And any hero you have, did or does that as well. And they get other people to help with that and work together as a close knit team. Men and women can work together and help each other and *become very close* by doing so.

Relationships break down when people, because of jealousies or insecurities, try to control or limit what their partners can have, while trying to get more for themselves. There is no win in marriage unless there is a win-win. Marriages start out win-win and they can continue that way. What good is it to have a long relationship if it's not going to be a happy one? If you fear helping your partner to succeed it's probably related to a fear that you will no longer be needed once he does. Fear of abandonment is a very deep-seated fear for many people. But, helping your partner will make you more valuable, not less. The more valuable you are to your partner, the less likely you are to be abandoned. So don't try to censor ideas at the organization stage. Bad dreams and desires have a way of dying on their own once we run into the realities of them.

Accepting Ideas

Good parents, as you know, listen to their kids dreams without criticism, no matter how unrealistic the dream. "I want to live on mars when I grow up and make 500 foot tall robots!" "Hey, that sounds like fun," dad says. What do good spouses do? The same thing. Some men want a flower garden. Some women want to be CEO of their own cosmetic empire. And then, some men do that, and women, too. Behind each man and woman who achieves are helpful people who supported their achievement. The same joy and excitement of watching children grow and blossom can be experienced watching a spouse grow and blossom. Sometimes dreams are mutual—"I want to do that," "Me too!" Many couples have discovered after many years, that the dream they have kept hidden is the same dream their partner has.

What do you do if your partner has a wild and crazy dream? Support it. When you love each other, neither of you will have a dream which shuts the other person out. If a dream really is bad for the relationship, your partner will give it up when that fact hits home (because of reality, not because of your control). Why? Because as a supportive wife, you will be more important to him. He can find another dream, but he can't find another you. Become controlling and negative, insecure and jealous, or develop an "I told you so" attitude, and you will become easy to replace, little different from many other women. If you behave like a low value wife, his desires will become more valuable to him than you are. In that case, even if he stays with you, he won't be happy. But trusting, feeling secure, and accepting will tighten the marriage bond. Exercise equipment and failed ventures will come and go, and that's ok when you have each other. No politician wins every election. Not every boy can be an astronaut.

Dreams and plans can be simple or elaborate. One couple's dreams may be a big screen TV and a new sofa. For another, a log cabin in the woods. For another, starting their own business. Or separate businesses. One can travel and one can stay home if it fits their dreams. That's right. Many couples have different interests, and even lifestyles, but they support each other, and enjoy their relationships and their lives. Relationships can be as varied as the people who are in them. It is very, very, exciting. Make one that suits you and your husband.

After Sharing Comes Planning

If your dreams are not complicated, you and your husband may naturally move into planning in order to start working on them. If your husband's dream is to plant a flower garden and yours is to take singing lessons, you will hardly need any more help. If you and your husband get stuck because of planning difficulties (like figuring out how to balance kids, a career, and a bicycle trip across Europe), you could get some planning help from a coach, financial guru, or some other professional. Dreams only become unachievable when people can't figure out and take the steps to achieve them. Professionals such as coaches help people with that.

Growing Together, Even as Sunset Approaches

What happens if you get to the point where you just want to sit together on a porch swing or spend some time with the grandchildren? Well, if you have truly worked on your dreams, you will enjoy that swing, even if things didn't work out the way you planned. Trying and failing doesn't bring regret. Failing to try brings regret. It would be very sad to be at the end of your years, with regrets about things you have missed because you never tried. Or to resent your partner because of what you had to give up for the "sake of" the relationship. When you work together as partners, you won't regret it, even when things don't work out all that great. In the end, you will still have each other and still enjoy each other. Even good relationships eventually come to an end, though. A "goodbye" comes that we don't want to say. And then a new beginning. But the end is always hard. It's sad to say that now, but you need to realize it now. He won't be alive forever, and time is precious. Don't live in fear of that, but don't put it so far out of your mind that you waste today. It is our brief time together that makes it so valuable. (At the time I write this, more than 20,000 have lost their husbands, wives, girlfriends, and boyfriends in a tsunami, a giant wave they didn't expect when they got up that morning). No matter how, goodbye always comes too soon in a good relationship.

"Twenty years from now you will be more disappointed by the things that you didn't do than by the ones you did do. So throw off the bowlines. Sail away from the safe harbor. Catch the trade winds in your sails. Explore. Dream. Discover."

Mark Twain

ABOUT THE AUTHOR

Jack Ito, PhD is a licensed clinical psychologist and marriage coach specializing in reconciling separated, emotionally detached, and high conflict marriages. "Coach Jack" offers hope and practical solutions to couples of all ages in more than 14 countries around the globe. "Regardless of a man or woman's age, income, beliefs, or number of fingers and toes, everyone has the desire to love and be loved by someone. Making sure that happens is my life's work." With the help of modern technologies and the latest advances in professional coaching, Coach Jack uses down to earth examples to take people, wherever they live, from a troubled relationship to a happy one.

Coach Jack specializes in not just creating interventions, but supporting and talking people through them so they can save relationships that otherwise would end. "I cannot physically go into their home and do the interventions for them. They are the only ones in the world who can make their relationships better. But, I can help them to sort out the trouble, get on the right path, and do what is *necessary* if they are ever going to have the kind of relationship they want to have. Once they are willing to do what is necessary, their success is practically guaranteed. The problem with most relationships is that people spend too much time doing what is *unnecessary* before they are ready to do what is necessary." Coach Jack even welcomes clients who have been recommended to break up or divorce by other professionals.

Coach Jack grew up in a small town in Vermont, in a family devastated by abuse and emotional conflict. "My father was a violent and insecure man; my mother was a loving, but dependent housewife who spent her days wishing she had never married him. There was no one who could help us to be a family. They just told my mother to leave him, and she couldn't bring herself to do that. Now, I realize he was as much a victim of his behaviors as she was. Neither of them knew what or how to do what was necessary to bring peace and love into their relationship. It's my intention to never let people I coach be left without a way to improve their relationship."

Coach Jack earned his doctorate in clinical psychology as well as a masters degree in theology from Fuller Theological Seminary in Pasadena, California. He has held positions as college professor, clinic director, specialist for the US Navy and Marine Corps, as well as marriage coach/consultant for numerous churches and Christian organizations. His formal training in coaching is from MentorCoach LLC.

Coach Jack now travels the world coaching, writing, and speaking. He lives with his wife, and maintains homes in the United States and Japan. His passion is people and relationships. You can find more information about Coach Jack as well as more marriage and relationship advice on his website at **coachjackito.com**.

INDEX

ALSO BY COACH JACK

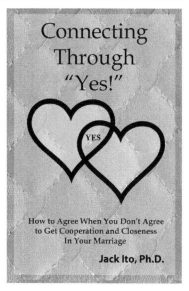

Connecting Through "Yes!"
How to Agree When You Don't Agree to Get
Cooperation and Closeness in Your Marriage
(2013) 292 pages

Do you know how to use agreement to transform your biggest areas of marital conflict into closeness, cooperation, and the changes that YOU want in your relationship?

In Connecting Through "Yes!" Marriage and Relationship Coach Jack Ito shows you with clear, easy to follow examples, how to positively communicate about the <u>biggest</u> problems that couples face. These are the same techniques his coaching clients use to reconcile marriages, end affairs, deal with addicted spouses, solve problems, end blaming, improve dating, handle money issues, and much more.

Available at online bookstores in paperback or as a downloadable Kindle eBook from Amazon.com